INTERNATIONAL FOOTBALL BOOK

No. 13

England captain Bobby Moore tackles Scotland's John O'Hare during an international match between the two countries.

INTERNATIONAL FOOTBALL BOOK

No. 13

Edited by Stratton Smith

Contributing Editors:

PETER JONES, ERIC BATTY

and PHILIP RISING

with contributions by

SIR MATT BUSBY ALAN BALL

LUIGI RIVA GEORGE BEST MORDECAI SPIEGLER

GORDON BANKS PAT JENNINGS BOB WILSON

BRIAN GLANVILLE JAIRZINHO LADISLAV PETRAS

TERRY HENNESSEY OVE KINDVALL IAN HUTCHINSON

BRYAN ROBSON ANATOLI BYCHEWECZ GRAHAM MOORE

CLYDE BEST LAU VAN RAVENS

KAMAMOTO TEOFILO CUBILLAS

GORDON JEFFERY

SOUVENIR PRESS LTD · LONDON

First published in 1971 by Souvenir Press Ltd., 95 Mortimer Street, London, W.1, and simultaneously in Canada by J. M. Dent & Son Ltd., Toronto.

ISBN 0 285 62014 2

Printed in Great Britain by
Sir Joseph Causton & Sons Ltd., London and Eastleigh.

CONTENTS

CONTENTS

LIST OF ILLUSTRATIONS

LIST OF ILLUSTRATIONS—*continued*

F.A. AND LEAGUE GET-TOGETHER

by SIR MATT BUSBY

IT would be a sad day for soccer if there was ever a serious split between the Football League and the Football Association.

I don't think a situation would ever develop to this extent, but nevertheless, it is true to say that over the years there has been growing friction between the two bodies that control our great game.

And I believe that now is the time to act before small differences can grow into a radical rift, which is why I was delighted to see discussions started this last 12 months to examine the various responsibilities of FA and League.

One newspaper referred to the issue at the time as a "bloodless revolution". Well, this may be a rather colourful way of expressing it, but it had to be recognised that there was a good deal of unrest among many League clubs at the way the authority has been split between League and FA.

The pressure for talks between the two organisations came from the representatives of two or three clubs at the annual meeting of the Football League during the summer of 1970.

And what I found most encouraging was that the Football Association who, of course, have the ultimate authority and responsibility for soccer generally, immediately agreed to discuss the situation with the League.

The result was that a joint committee was set up representing the FA and League in equal numbers and together they have been trying to solve the problems that have been worrying the clubs for some time.

These problems cover issues such as finance,

Sir Matt Busby, one of soccer's most respected administrators, is a regular contributor to the International Football Book.

(Left) Brian Kidd of Manchester United heads for goal despite the challenge of Liverpool captain Tommy Smith. The result? A goal for United. (Above) Pat Crerand of Manchester United takes on Leeds United's Terry Cooper with Tony Dunne and Carlo Sartori in attendance.

discipline and international matches, but basically what it boils down to is whether the League should have more control of its affairs as they affect the professional League clubs.

Personally, I think the time has come when the League should have more direct say in the running of its competitions and the administration of the clubs.

I don't say this with any disrespect for the Football Association, who after all have nurtured this game of ours since before the Football League competition was formed and they have been responsible for fostering our links with the rest of the world through international matches–the World Cup in latter years.

They have also done a magnificent job in ensuring that in matters like the rules we have all been treading along the same road with the result that the game played in Madrid is by and large the one played in Manchester and even East and West can meet in more harmony than the politicians can manage!

But at the same time football at professional level has gradually been moving into a more complex business while the Football Association has to concern itself also with the vast numbers of amateurs who play soccer, as well as the numerous competitions involving semi-professionals and part-timers.

It seems to me that we have reached a stage in development when the League must have more control of its affairs and be in a stronger position to make reforms which have been needed for some time but which have been remote to the FA, whose Council is made up of many amateur club representatives as well as League members.

One of the new areas in which the Football League has been active in the last year has been sponsored football and I was glad Manchester United were able to take part in the Watney Cup, the first venture into "commercialised soccer".

The most capped player in the world . . . Bobby Charlton, pictured with just a few of the full international caps he has won for England. Bobby passed Billy Wright's record of 105 during the 1970 World Cup finals in Mexico.

For years football resisted the idea of commerce and industry subsidising our sport by putting money into the game and then perhaps influencing it in some way or other. I think we simply did not like the idea of someone else sticking their nose into what we considered our business!

Perhaps that was the right outlook and a healthy policy in the early days, but times change and I think it sensible that soccer should now be prepared to examine the ideas of people who are willing to put money into the game in return for having their names associated with some aspect of it.

One must not go to ridiculous extremes of course; I would hate to see a game of football stopped every quarter of an hour to carry a plug for someone's product on the lines of a television programme!

But I cannot see soccer being carried away by the thought of cash to succumb to crazy ideas like that. The Watney people for instance were most dignified and sensible about their advertising campaign and what they expected from football in return for the money they put into the game.

I would like Manchester United to win the Ford Sporting League sometime and the Texaco Cup also brought a lot of welcome cash into the game.

And with more authority to plan our future, more control of its own affairs, I believe the Football League can lead us into many more productive spheres as soccer measures up to the 'Seventies.

Captains do more than call 'Heads' or 'Tails'

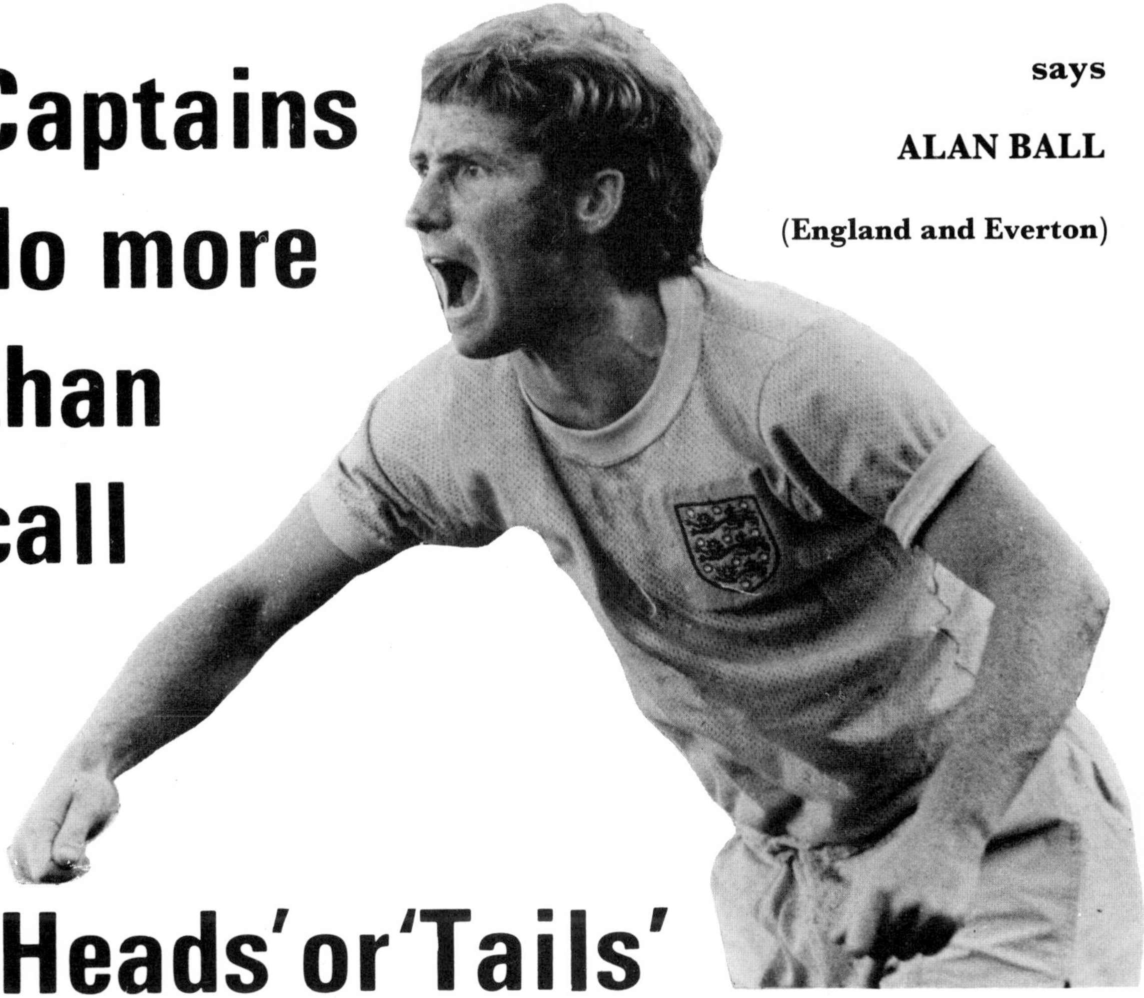

says

ALAN BALL

(England and Everton)

THERE'S no point trying to hide the fact that when I was a youngster, during my formative years as a professional footballer, I was a bit of a handful. Maybe my highly-publicised moments of bad temper came because I tried to live up to the reputation given people with red hair–or maybe the hair simply made me easier to single out on the pitch.

Or maybe it stemmed from what was really a deliberate gimmick, created by my father and I. My gimmick was simply to develop a real Ball of fire approach–to run and run, non-stop, always buzzing here and there through the whole ninety minutes of a game.

The more involved with play, the more likely you are to attract trouble. And trouble and I seemed to be inseparable for several seasons.

I was bawled out by Ron Suart when he was manager of Blackpool. I'd argued against a referee's decision and was booked and Mr. Suart told me, in no uncertain terms, that I was in danger of letting the team down–that other clubs were fast seeing that I was easy to needle, especially in the thick of battle.

There was newspaper talk of me having feuds with certain players–like Bryan Douglas, of Blackburn Rovers, and Billy Bremner, of Leeds. And I was sent off during an England Under-23 game in Austria. I unashamedly cried after that incident, which anyway was followed by a fatherly chat from

Sir Alf Ramsey, who told me that I simply had to learn to accept decisions, even bad decisions, by referees.

All that was a long time ago. For a while, I even tried to play a sort of softer game, get away from the non-stop buzzing, but it wasn't really me. I simply had to be involved in the game, whether for Everton or England. I wanted to be the best player in the world and I took my inspiration from stars like Denis Law and Jimmy Greaves.

Ambition is important to a footballer. I swore to my dad, perhaps my greatest supporter in the game, that I'd be an England player before I was twenty, and I made it with just a few months to go.

So I was once the bad boy. Though it was a tremendous fight against an obviously suspect temperament, I improved my behaviour. I came to realise that I was the one out of step, not everybody else.

Now the point of this preamble is simply this. At the beginning of last season, I was made club captain of Everton. When Mr. Harry Catterick, the manager, told me that I'd be the skipper, it was one of the proudest moments of my life.

It meant that the past had been forgotten and forgiven. That I was considered now to be a leader of men. A captain. It meant more to me than it would to the normal player who had no bad past to live down.

After all, many people had figured that I wasn't responsible enough to "captain" myself, let alone a team of First Division footballers. Yet I'd always had this confidence that one day I'd do just that.

What angers me is the theory that a club captain in this day and age has virtually nothing to do.

Alan Ball in action for England against Malta in Valetta. England won 1–0 with a goal from Martin Peters.

Maybe call "heads" or "tails" and leave it at that. The argument is that everything is so highly organised that nothing is left to chance out there on the park.

I think this is an argument littered with rubbish.

You have to have one man entirely responsible for translating the pre-match ideas into actual match action. The manager can do his talking before a game, and at half-time, and that's the end of his involvement. The captain, too, has a great responsibility towards young players–lads having their first taste of First Division action.

You nurse them along. Spot weaknesses and try to put them right, at the moment, not a few hours afterwards.

But a good skipper's job doesn't end on the field of play. He is, essentially, the link between the players and the management. He certainly shouldn't get involved in business matters like contracts and so on, but things like allocation of tickets for players, matters of welfare, they all come within his duties.

In other words, I regard it as being a very responsible job indeed–one to be taken seriously. And anyone who thinks it's pretty much a mere formality doesn't know what it entails.

A model captain also has to have that whole aura of authority. Football followers with longer memories talk of how good at the job was Stan Cullis, dominating all things with strength and power in the middle of the Wolverhampton Wanderers' defence. There was Joe Mercer, too, now a manager but a magnificent captain in his final seasons with Arsenal.

But the captains of today are good, too. My model captain, as it were, is Bobby Moore. I know his powers through playing alongside him in the England team, but he is also dominant with West Ham. The Hammers, with all that talent, remain very much an enigma–it's hard to see how they can have so little success with so much ability. But one cannot blame the immaculate Bobby Moore for the failings.

Bobby is a great captain because he uses his experience to help others and to marshal things when the game isn't going well. He has obvious positional sense and strength in the tackle and so on

A player and captain admired by Alan Ball . . . Bobby Moore of West Ham United and England.

(Left) Allan Clarke of Leeds United and England is beaten in the air by Crystal Palace centre half John McCormick. (Right) Ian Ure of Manchester United clears from Derby County outside left Alan Hinton.

–the ability to go forward when the time is right. He inspires other players because of his own skills and his calmness. To be a steadying influence is another important aspect of the captain's job–keeping his head, in fact, while all around him are losing theirs.

Not so long after I was made captain of Everton, I was selected to skipper the Football League representative side, but unfortunately missed the game because of injury.

That was a bitter disappointment, but I feel that time is on my side. It was nice to read suggestions that I was being "nursed" along with the possible idea of later skippering the full England side. Obviously, that is something I can't really comment upon.

But I'll make no bones about my sheer ambitiousness. I wanted to captain my club, and I always had the idea at the back of my head that I'd achieve just that. Having had a taste of captaincy, my natural instinct is to build my ambition for the future on the highest aims.

To lead out an England side, preferably at Wembley, must be the biggest thrill of them all. I've had my share of excitement in my travels round the world, but to be captain of England is an honour that it is impossible to take too lightly.

They may do things differently at other clubs, but the captaincy at Everton is a highly-prized job. I've really worked at learning the way to handle team-mates and to do things the right way.

Which is why I just can't help laughing when I hear those characters say that skippering a top club is just a formality. You try running a team with eleven captains, or no captain at all–just see how far you get.

Besides, it gives me a chance to have a word with referees at official level!

England's Bobby Charlton shoots for goal with Dave Powell of Wales endeavouring to challenge.

LUIGI RIVA

GOAL-HUNGRY BUT...A MONSTER!

by
LUIGI RIVA

(Italy and Cagliari)

IN Italy the newspapermen call me "The Monster" apparently because of my speed and shooting power. I'm not sure whether I like the title or not but I'm stuck with it after I was described like that by Aldo Biscardi, the sports editor of the paper "Paese Sera" which is published in Rome.

Signor Biscardi wrote a book about me, too, but I shouldn't complain about the press. Most of the time they are just like anybody else, doing their job the best way they can. Anyway they've been kind to me in other ways–two years in a row giving me the first prize for Italy's best player.

There are other kinds of newspapermen, however, and some of them known as the *paparazzis* I certainly don't like. Now and again they give me special treatment, following me everywhere I go. They did it in 1968, following me constantly for two solid weeks. What they were after was a photo of me, preferably in a nightclub kissing a girl. Any girl–even just a little "peck" on the cheek would have been enough for them.

Sometimes these *paparazzis* are referred to as the black-mail photographers and this description is not far wrong. When it was my turn, I was followed everywhere by at least one photographer but often I managed to shake them off my tail. Sometimes I think, even against double-marking, it's easier to score goals than it is to get a little privacy, but they were certainly wasting their time following me.

I'm not much of a talker and I hardly ever read. I gave up reading books when I was still at school, always too busy thinking about football. Maybe I should have set a better example, I don't know. But most of my class-mates copied me and probably some of them have lived to regret not working harder at their studies.

But I have no regrets–even after two broken legs. I've made plenty of money and hope to make more. I earn about £60,000 a year and most of it just goes in the bank, and when I have a holiday–a break from training and football, I nearly always spend it visiting my mother.

In Italy football is probably more important than anything else–even politics. How else can you explain the fact that in a gallup poll in 1969 to find out the most popular person in Italy I came out in top place? Even Sophia Loren was only second and the President of the State was well down the list.

Italian football is said abroad to be the roughest and toughest, but that doesn't fit with my experiences. I've had two broken legs–playing for Italy against Portugal and Austria. And even the "marking" in Italy isn't the tightest or dirtiest I've experienced. I'm described as a "monster" but some of the alleged "tackling" I've experienced against foreign teams is terrible.

I've been really disillusioned about the supposed sportsmanship of some other football countries. The Swedes, for example, are said to be amateurs, supposed to play for pleasure rather than money or success. But in my opinion the Swedes ruined their reputation in the last World Cup in Mexico.

When we played them in Toluca they had three men "marking" me. Boxing me in whenever they could. But they won't go very far with these kind of tactics and, in fact, although I didn't score in that

(Below) Tottenham Hotspur wing half Phil Beal makes a successful clearance with Ray Kennedy of Arsenal close at hand. (Right) the unmistakable style and determination of Luigi Riva, playing against Brazil.

Pelikan
ERALDO

Luigi Riva, of Cagliari and Italy–an idol in Sardinia and practically everywhere else in Italy.

game, it was their decision to put three men on me that led to their defeat.

I was a bit disappointed not to have scored in this game for it was the first time that I failed to get a goal when playing for Italy. Certainly it wasn't a clean game. We won all right but it wasn't a victory to be happy about. My three "watchdogs" were strong and aggressive and the English referee John Taylor let them do what they wanted to me.

They obstructed me, held me, knocked me down and attacked me from behind. I was in good shape and the altitude at Toluca didn't bother me but though I got three or four good passes I had no chance to score. My "guards" saw to that.

Even so the Swedes made big mistakes–one of them being to concentrate too much on me. In doing so, putting three men on me they left too much room for Sandro Mazzola. He's a great player with football in his blood. At home we call him the "brain" because he has the outstanding ability to play the ball with his feet and look around and think at the same time!

It was Mazzola who made our goal scored by my Cagliari club-mate Angelo Domenghini. The Swedes played much too slowly and their way of shooting is antique. Also they have no imagination, little skill and are much too slow, playing without any change in pace or rhythm. They had one good player though, their centre forward Ove Kindvall but because of his team's concentration in defence and on me especially, he got very little support. And what Kindvall needs is low passes to his feet but in the game against us he didn't get any!

Mexico was a strange experience looking back. For one thing, except for the quarter final match we played against Mexico, the home fans gave us tremendous support in our early games. In Toluca they chanted "It-al-ia, ra-ra-ra" and when we asked why afterwards we were told it was because our flag is red, white and green–the same colours as that of Mexico.

In the end, of course, we were beaten by Brazil in the final and to some extent at least I feel that we contributed to our own downfall because we were too sure of ourselves. After the way we'd played in the semi-finals against Germany the atmosphere changed, discipline was tightened and everything became too regimented.

Inside our hotel, the *Parco dos Principes*, which was a motel-type hotel with little bungalows, the players were kept under guard. Outside the hotel were armed police in the last days before the final and no one was allowed to get in without an official pass. And the guards said openly that they would use their guns if anyone failed to observe the "No Entry" sign.

Inside the hotel, each little bungalow was like a concrete bunker from a World War movie. Inside each one were players–let out several times a day but only for training, feeding and collecting mail from home.

EUROPEAN COMPETITION ESSENTIAL

says
GEORGE BEST

(N. Ireland and Manchester United)

THOUGH I'm as proud as Punch when I step out for a Northern Ireland international in Belfast, though I'm sure I have the words 'Manchester United' engraved on my heart for League and Cup games at Old Trafford–I honestly don't think I'm the completely happy footballer if there is no European football.

I know the English First Division is the hardest competition in the world and even though I'm only half-way through my career, I have a few books' worth of memories of games in it. But cut off my supply of European contests and I feel somehow incomplete.

You get into Europe by doing well in other competitions. Either the League, or the FA Cup, or through the Fairs Cup set-up and so on. Through not doing so well, and through one bit of bother at Old Trafford, we had a couple of seasons with no European excitement. It was hard to take.

Nothing will ever erase, for instance, the emotional memories of the night we won the European Cup, after years of effort, before 100,000 wildly excited fans at Wembley Stadium.

Maybe it took a lot of the average supporters a long time to appreciate the vital importance of success in Europe, but the players always knew what a morale-booster it was. The European Cup started in 1956, but it wasn't until 1967 that a British team won the competition. Celtic first, then a year later Manchester United.

There was the excitement of the semi-finals against Real Madrid. And the 4–1 beating, after extra time, of Benfica at Wembley. Benfica had won the trophy twice before. Real Madrid had won it six times, and been runners-up on two other occasions. So we hardly had the easiest of passages through.

Even now I still tingle with excitement at the thought of European competition. Yet I didn't manage many happy memories of my first trip abroad as a youngster. We were off to Lisbon for a

quarter-final match against Sporting Club in the European Cup-winners' Cup. We were 4–1 from the first leg.

In the second leg we were a goal down inside a minute, Tony Dunne unluckily conceding a penalty. And we were three down at half-time. We lost. Lost more than just the result, too, even though we managed to pull ourselves together on our return to beat Tottenham Hotspur in a League game at White Hart Lane.

That was a good season for me personally. People were talking about me. Some even compared me with a young Stanley Matthews or a junior Tom Finney. People who knew what soccer was all about warned me that I wouldn't find it so easy in future–not once the professionals knew what I could do. And most certainly it hasn't been so easy since.

Despite the attentions of two Tottenham Hotspur players, the mercurial George Best succeeds in finding a way through on behalf of Manchester United at White Hart Lane.

I was dropped from the United side, and vowed it would never happen again. I found the marking got tighter. And as the seasons passed by, I got more than my share of the headlines for being in trouble with referees.

Perhaps I bored people by saying that I expected rather more protection from referees. I didn't think the game was getting progressively dirtier, or anything, but as I counted the bruises after each game I knew that opponents were leaning harder and harder on me. There was no use squealing, because it is all part of the game of football.

I hope I never squeal. I talked about 'protection', though, because it was partly my explanation for my wretched outbursts against authority. Against linesmen, referees, that feeling of frustration grew and grew.

The headlines–'Best at the Cross-roads' . . . 'Best in Trouble Again' . . . 'Best, Genius in Danger of Blowing Up His Career' . . . you take notice of that kind of thing. You think you'll never lose your temper again. But in the sudden flare-up in a flashpoint dispute in the thick of battle–well, it's not so easy to keep total control. Opponents learned how to niggle me. There were other players–no names no pack drill–who had also had their share of trouble in their early days.

They gave me advice on how to curb myself. But I'd actually got through the early seasons with no trouble at all to speak of. It was only after six or seven years of extra-close attention from defenders that I started flaring up. Of course, people interpreted this as meaning I'd got a rapidly-swollen head. Others inferred that I regarded myself as being somehow bigger than the game itself.

It was never true. Maybe it was that Irish temperament that made me enjoy European football against the Latins. Perhaps I felt instinctively that they reacted in much the same way as I did. Though the South Americans of Estudiantes, against whom we played in the World Club championship, were much too petty for me . . . the shirt-tugging, hair-pulling, pinching all got me down. I'd taken a lot when eventually I was sent off over one incident at Old Trafford in the second leg.

At any rate, I cherish my memories of European contests. After that Sporting Club fiasco, and after

No mistaking this character . . . a typical shot of Dave Mackay, the irrepressible skipper of Derby County.

I'd been dropped from the United first team, we started again in the European Cup. I got a couple, I remember, on my return against Helsinki JK and felt much better about my future in the game.

A win over Vorwaerts got us through to the last eight. Then came Benfica, early in 1966. We won 3–2 and it would have been more if Eusebio hadn't saved one of his genius touches for late in the game.

And there was the return game. It's history now that Paddy Crerand, in the dressing-room before the kick-off, smashed a ball accidentally into a mirror–and we had that feeling we were on the start of seven years' bad luck. In fact, we walloped and humiliated and thumped Benfica that night, by 5–1. And they, only a goal down remember, were fielding the Portuguese front line of Augusto, Eusebio, Torres, Coluna and Simoes.

With all modesty, I must say I had a pretty good game, with a couple of goals and one of those matches where everything you try comes off. Alas, we didn't get much further that year. But the triumph was yet to come.

So now I go into the second half of my career. I've had all the excitement and the honours–European Footballer of the Year, Footballer of the Year, that European Cup medal and so on. Unfortunately, because of this temperament of mine, I've also rowed myself into the sort of headlines that no player wants.

It's obvious that I've got to concentrate all the time on holding myself in check. It's easy to say that I should change my attitude. I doubt very much whether many people can summon up a completely different personality change just at will.

I get hammered from behind maybe fifty times and then something snaps on the fifty-first. Don't ask me why it happens. I don't want people to feel sorry for me–but it would help if some of my detractors (at personal level, I mean, rather than at footballing level) could just try to understand that I am what I am. That if there is a spark in me, it can affect me badly as well as in a good way.

And let's keep the European competitions rolling. I think we'll get more of them as the world itself gets even smaller.

(Left) one of England's most tenacious and versatile players–Emlyn Hughes of Liverpool. (Right) Derby County captain Dave Mackay holds aloft the Watney Cup. With him is Sir Stanley Rous.

Israel's World Cup star

MORDECAI SPIEGLER

talks of

HIS TRAVELS AND OFFERS

ISRAEL'S 1970 World Cup bid was never a serious challenge to the leading soccer nations of the World, but for the players who took part it was a long and tiring journey that four times took us half way round the World. Our qualification campaign really began with the 1968 Olympic Games soccer series in Mexico where we reached the quarter finals and with just a touch of luck might have done even better.

This was against what we might call 'medium' strength national squads for in the Olympics, players who have taken part in any earlier World Cup are automatically barred by the rules.

In 1968 we reached the Olympics quarter finals where we drew 1–1 against Bulgaria–even after an extra 30 minutes and then while Israel went out on

Mordecai Spiegler, pictured wearing a West Ham shirt. But he never got to wear one in a Football League match.

the toss of a coin, the Bulgarians went on to reach the final.

Our team which played in the 1968 Olympics was pretty well the basis of our World Cup squad and after returning to Israel we were determined to go back to Mexico in 1970. To achieve this aim we had to play qualifying matches in South Korea and then, after flying back home, we took off again for Australia and the final play-off.

In Sydney, we spent most of the game hanging on to the 1–0 lead we'd gained at home and near the end a really great ball from our inside right, Giora Spiegel, eluded the entire Australian defence, and there I was all alone with only the Australian 'keeper to beat. My goal seemed to spur the Australians on to even greater efforts but luckily for us they only managed one goal–and we were set for Mexico again.

For Israel this really was an achievement. Though we had every encouragement from the Israeli Government–which administrates the entire spectrum of sport in our country and invests at least US $1 million every year in sport and new facilities –every one of our players was a real amateur and forced by circumstances to keep football third in his priorities . . . without even thinking of any kind of family life. With the Middle East situation always unsettled I had to do 2½ years' National Service as a soldier when I was 18 and this is currently running at three years a man.

By force of circumstances all Israelis are soldiers first; then we can think of our jobs and thirdly . . . football.

At home, football is clearly the most popular sport with 500 clubs and more than 10,000 active players from a population of less than three million. In the season we play on average two games a week but, of course, not in Mexican type conditions.

Strangely enough, in spite of the different political situation which surrounds our country we have proved that Jews and Arabs **can and do** live and play together. Though foreigners might find it difficult to believe we have an entirely Arab club playing in our Second Division–Bney Nazareth (Sons of Nazareth in English)–and, take it from me, every game is played out without thought of politics, just like any other club and any other league.

Once we had qualified for the final stages of the World Cup there was a considerable period during which we all seemed to be over-awed. Many of the World's best teams gathered in Mexico and, practically without experience at top level, we were understandably perhaps nervous and worried.

Mordecai Spiegler did play for West Ham during his short stay at Upton Park but only in non-competitive matches.

After losing only 2–0 against Uruguay we seemed to become more confident. After the game we saw the match on television and suddenly I found my feelings of inferiority had gone. I sensed my colleagues felt this too. Before the next match against Sweden I remember thinking quite clearly to myself. "OK, they are Swedish and they've got Kindvall and Axelsson but so what? I've got two feet and one head . . . the same as them. Let's have a go". The result was an encouraging 1–1 draw that I'm sure will give future Israeli teams both incentive and encouragement when they meet teams adjudged to be superior.

Not a line up of show-girls but a defence wall as illustrated by West Ham. Yet despite their combined efforts the ball managed to find a way past skipper Bobby Moore (6) while Peter Eustace (8) cannot bear to watch.

Four days later we got another draw against Italy, but it must be admitted right away they were fish of a very different kind. Our outside chance of a place in the last eight kept us going but Italy had only to draw to qualify and they knew it. Even so, while we tried to slow the game with short passing the Italians scored one goal (disallowed for off-side) and another shot hit a post. But I fluffed a great chance to score just before half time. Through on my own, going into the Italian penalty area, I had the ball at my feet and only goalkeeper Albertosi to beat. From up in the stand it might have looked like a sitter.

In the thousandth of a second that makes the difference between goals and missed chances, Albertosi shifted his weight towards his right hand post and by automatic response I shot at once . . . to his left. Spectators might have seen this differently, but I'm sure I did the right thing. Albertosi had gone the wrong way–but he'd left his feet behind–and as I shot his left leg came out to turn the ball away from goal. For my money, Albertosi is quite a goalkeeper.

After the World Cup I had several new offers to join professional clubs. Though we travelled an awful lot between 1968 and 1970 it seems to me I've spent half my life on the move and I would have loved to become a professional. To start with I was born in Russia, in a town called Azbest amongst the Ural mountains in the East, just a few months before the end of the last war. When I was a year old my parents moved to Germany and from there they had two chances to emigrate–the U.S.A. and Israel. Finally in 1950 they chose Israel.

I had another chance to go to the U.S.A. in 1968 when I was 23. This opportunity arose when the

Americans tried to introduce professional football, but I turned that down. Looking back I did the right thing. Then in 1969 I was invited to England and spent a few days in Birmingham where Tommy Docherty was at that time manager of Aston Villa. I was eager to join Villa but the Israeli FA refused to sanction my transfer and that ended it.

Similar opportunities arose after the World Cup in Mexico where I had offers from clubs in England, Germany, the U.S.A. and France. FC Nantes were really eager to engage me–their club President and I almost shared the same shadow in Mexico after Israel had been knocked out, but again . . . no permission. I would have liked to go–not for money but for satisfaction, because I'm sure that everyone who plays football dreams of the chance to become a professional and I would dearly have liked to find out if I was good enough.

Don't count me out of 1974 says

GORDON BANKS

(England and Stoke City)

ONE goal made all the difference to England's chance of winning the World Cup in Mexico and in my opinion it wasn't any of the three goals West Germany scored in the quarter final in Leon. The real key–the difference between success and failure–is difficult to explain to anyone who didn't experience the conditions in Mexico, but the heat, the altitude and the travelling involved were tremendous problems. My goal–the one that in my opinion really led to England's elimination–was the one that Jairzinho put past me in the England-Brazil match in the Jalisco Stadium in Guadalajara.

(Left) Joe Corrigan, Manchester City goalkeeper, seems to be heading the ball into his own net, with Gerry Ingram of Nottingham Forest, in support. But in fact Corrigan had pushed the ball over the bar. (Right) Chris Lawler of Liverpool is beaten to a corner by Gordon Banks of Stoke City during a match at Anfield.

Gordon Banks spends many hours practising his art and is quick to point out that there is no substitute for hard work.

Losing 1-0 to Brazil inevitably meant that they won our group and under the rules stayed to play their quarter final at Jalisco against Peru.

This was the real deciding factor, for pushed into second place in the Guadalajara Group we had to travel to Leon and take on West Germany. Five hours' travelling in a coach the day before a vital World Cup game is not my idea of the ideal way to prepare for a big game. It wouldn't have been pleasant anywhere but in the heat of Mexico we all suffered. We hardly had time to get settled down in our new headquarters and hotel before the game was on top of us and the Germans, of course, staying 'at home' in their quarters near Leon had a big advantage in this respect.

I'm sure that before the vital England-Brazil match, the Brazilians would have been quite happy to settle for a goal-less draw. We were both in the same position hoping to do well in the series and knowing that we were the favourites to take the top two places in Guadalajara and so reach the quarter finals. Looking back, I feel both teams didn't want to lose and equally didn't want to take too much out of themselves physically with so many more games to come. Certainly we had a great game with Brazil, giving at least as good as we got, but Brazil scored the only goal. I'm sure they felt themselves to be just a little fortunate to have won 1–0 just as we would, perhaps, have felt the same if the result had gone the other way.

Losing to Brazil, and having to travel to Leon for the quarter final, made all the difference for I'm positive that if we'd stayed in Guadalajara, and met Peru, we would have gone on to the semi finals. Of course, we would still have had to meet Brazil in the final and though they were obviously outstanding against Italy I think we would have given Brazil a better game. They beat us in Guadalajara but meeting us again in the final could have been very different.

Mexico itself posed unusual problems and overall I feel the England lads did very well. The climate, food, everything was stacked against the European teams and although the altitude didn't prove to be such a physical problem as did the heat, the ball doesn't fly 'true' when you get up at around 8,000 to 9,000 feet above sea level.

I'd already discovered this in our pre-World Cup games in Ecuador and Colombia. In the rarefied atmosphere at such altitudes the ball comes at you much quicker than it does at home. It was such a big problem as we had discovered before arriving in Mexico, that we were already getting in as much shooting practice as we could. But even when the World Cup games began we hadn't really become accustomed to the things the ball could do in the air and you just had to watch it all the way. At first, shots just went whizzing past me before I'd moved or even thought of moving and it wasn't just the extra pace of the ball either. A fellow could shoot at you and you saw it all the way, then suddenly it could turn or dip late in flight even when it was right up on top of you–almost in your hands.

After the World Cup some people were surprised that I was left out of the England team–Peter Shilton played in the first game of last season against East Germany at Wembley–but it didn't surprise me at all. Looking at things logically, Sir Alf Ramsey has got to build a squad aimed at winning the World Cup back again in 1974 and bearing in mind that I'll be 35 when that series starts it's obvious that he's got to look about and give everyone their chance. There are plenty of good goalkeepers about in England, too, and few people know better than I just how good young Peter is–remember we were together at Leicester before I was transferred to Stoke City.

Another one of England's many brilliant goalkeepers . . . Peter Bonetti of Chelsea and so often the understudy to Banks in the international squad.

A great deal can happen in the next three years but believe me I'll be training and playing just as hard as ever and barring injury and accidents I hope to go on for some time yet. It's not a question of training harder as you get older–for goalkeepers it's different anyway because they aren't subject to the leg weariness that overcomes the outfield players in their middle thirties.

I've always trained hard and I don't think its possible to do more in this sense. Fitness has always mattered to me and I've always believed that the more effort you put into training the more you'll benefit when it comes to playing in matches. There isn't anything particular that I think helps me or has helped me in the past–just hard work. I remember I used to watch goalkeepers like Bert Trautmann and Bert Williams when I was young and picked up a great many tips watching them. This, and knowing what your weaknesses are and doing something about them, are what really matters with keeping goal.

Mentally a game can be just as tiring for a goalkeeper as anyone else but physically it's easier. As time goes by I'll probably cut out some of the longer runs I still do and concentrate more on body work and short sprints; but right at the heart of goalkeeping is the business of stopping the ball hitting the back of your net. Where I think I scored, looking back, was in realising when I was young that you had to work particularly hard at your weaknesses. For example, if a goalkeeper is weak on high crosses then he's got to devote extra time to this aspect of the game. I was very lucky in having teammates who were prepared to come back to the ground and help me do extra training in the afternoons, giving me the kind of balls I knew I needed to work at.

Of course, it isn't easy to predict when you are going to retire or how many years you have left in you but I don't see myself being finished for some time yet. I know very well that the competition for the England jersey is going to be really tough in 1974, but I reckon I'll still be around. Having

Pelé is a man who counts himself among Gordon Banks' greatest fans–and with good reason. Who will ever forget the save Banks made for England from a Pelé header in Mexico?

played in the World Cup Final and helped to win the trophy gives you an appetite–you want to do it again and that's exactly how I feel about 1974.

I'll be 35 at the time of the next World Cup but goalkeepers like Lev Yachin (Russia) and Antonio Carbarjal (Mexico) have played in international matches at forty, so that gives me a pretty big margin. Given ordinary luck I'll still be around and if Sir Alf chooses me–as of course I hope he will –I'll give him everything I've got.

With goalkeeping it's a bit different from other positions. As you get older you expect to be in the right place more and more often . . . doing the right thing. And, if you anticipate something wrongly or you find yourself out of position when someone's shooting at your goal, it's simply a question of getting in the way. This is how I've always felt about it–go for everything and hold on tight to everything you can. And if all else fails just get in the way and stop the ball, even if it hits you in the face.

Arsenal captain Frank McLintock, a Scottish international, wins possession from West Bromwich Albion striker Jeff Astle.

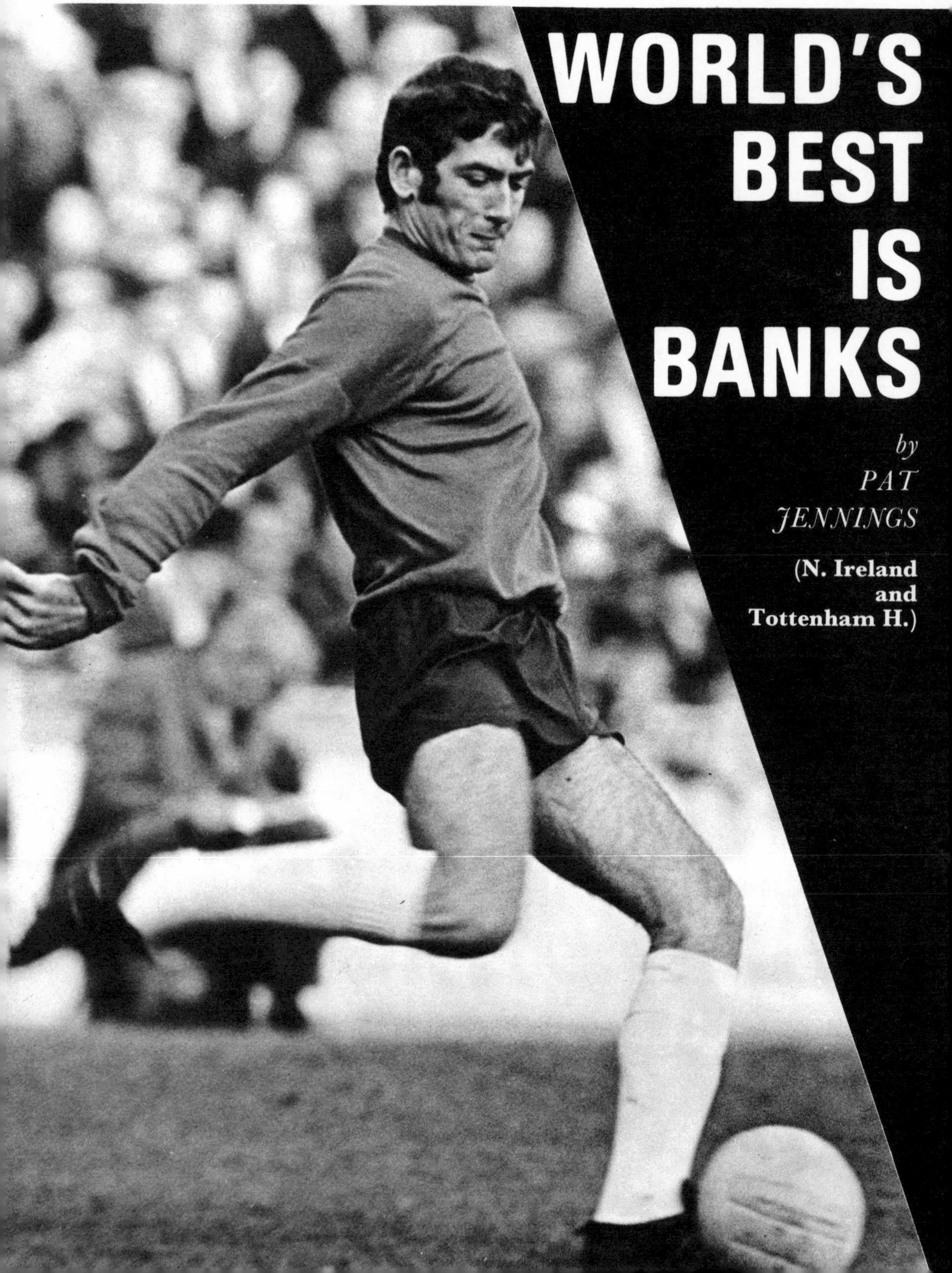

WORLD'S BEST IS BANKS

by
PAT JENNINGS

(N. Ireland and Tottenham H.)

THE World's best goalkeeper of the moment is, without doubt, England's Gordon Banks and I am quite sure that overall the standard of goalkeeping in Britain is far higher than anywhere else in the world. I would go further, and say that very often it is in goalkeeping that foreign teams are let down and with the possible exceptions of the Germans and Russians, who play more or less the same kind of game that we play, the vast majority of foreign goalkeepers would benefit enormously from continued exposure to the British game.

To put this another way, if I had to be the second choice goalkeeper with my club or if I was starting again as a youngster and had a choice of club, the team I would choose to join would be Stoke City. Naturally I prefer to stay where I am right now but if I had to be number two it would be Stoke that I would choose because it would give me a real good look at the way Gordon Banks works in training and copes with problems in matches. Let me just add one more point on this personal theme–in this hypothetical situation I would like Banks to be the age he is and me to be 17.

Personally, I love the high crosses. There's nothing I like better than facing a team with wingers or even only one winger for this means that they will probably rely on his ability to go down the line and cross the ball, no doubt hoping that something will develop. I'm sure this is one of the strongest points in my game, being able to take the high ball and if the opposition plugs away at throwing high crosses into my box I can take them all day and half the night. I love it.

The foreigners have good reactions and are very agile, too, but they let themselves down on the simple things like pushing away the high ball. This is why I'm sure that the vast majority of them would benefit from a prolonged period playing in Britain. Personally I dislike punching for a variety of reasons –for example if I go out and knock a ball down my colleagues are caught out of position and with the ball running loose I'm out of goal and anything can happen. On the other hand when I go out and take the ball, the game stops dead. There's no more

Tottenham Hotspur and Northern Ireland goalkeeper Pat Jennings safely collects a high cross.

danger with the ball in my hands and in addition my team-mates have time to push up and make new positions for themselves before I throw or kick the ball out to start an attack.

Punch or push the ball away and you can put the entire team in trouble whereas if you meet and keep the ball, it's easy for everyone. Confidence has a lot to do with it, of course, but I would certainly always prefer to try and catch it rather than punch the ball away.

One exception to this general opinion on foreign 'keepers is the Russian Yevgueni Rudakov who had a grand game for the USSR in Moscow when I played there for Ireland in a 1970 World Cup qualifying match. He's big–around 6′ 6″ I think–and brave, too. He took everything in the air that was thrown into the penalty area and he was very agile and good on the line. He made a couple of really good saves that day–and even more important he produced them at what could have been turning points in the match. If we'd scored we might have gone on to get a draw or even win and in my opinion it was him who turned the game in Russia's favour.

There's no big secret about taking high balls. My approach is simple. When I'm expecting a cross and the player on the ball is far enough away from you it gives you time to make up 10 or 12 yards to get there and reach the ball. In this situation I usually go out about five yards–from there I can get back on the line if the cross doesn't come–and if it does I'm already on my way.

Being pretty big, and always good at jumping, I reckon that being able to use my hands and arms I can beat anyone to a high ball and with the confidence that comes from doing it again and again

Pat Jennings in action for Spurs.

the rest is easy. You just get it, hold it and hang on, no matter how you come down. Sometimes you can finish up on your back or on your head, but getting the ball and hanging on to it is the big thing.

Of course, you dare not go out five yards in every situation, particularly if the player is around the 18 yard line and might have a go at goal himself. Then you've got to cover the near post shot–just in case–and a short, low centre driven in hard can cause real trouble. You can only go out with confidence to the long cross or long high ball that hangs in the air. The low cross, even head height I class as *low* because this invalidates the advantage I get from being able to jump and use my hands. In this kind of situation you just have to wait . . . and stay on your toes.

I'd say that being brought up in Ireland played a big part in schooling me for being a goalkeeper and coping with the high cross for though I played in youth football, the school I went to in Newry didn't

Two of England's finest young players, Steve Kember of Crystal Palace (left) and Steve Perryman of Tottenham Hotspur.

play soccer. There we all had to play Gaelic football –the game in which they use rugby posts and a soccer ball and score points. You get three points for scoring a soccer-type goal and one point for a 'rugby' goal that goes over the bar.

It's a mixture of rugby and soccer and although they do have 'keepers I played out on the field where you can either kick the ball or punch it, and the emphasis is on fielding high balls and kicking long passes ahead. The ball was in the air most of the time and outfield it was all 'getting up' and jumping with players *all around you.*

Of course, they only play the game in Ireland but this is a great pity from the viewpoint of a Continental goalkeeper. If they could play the Gaelic game

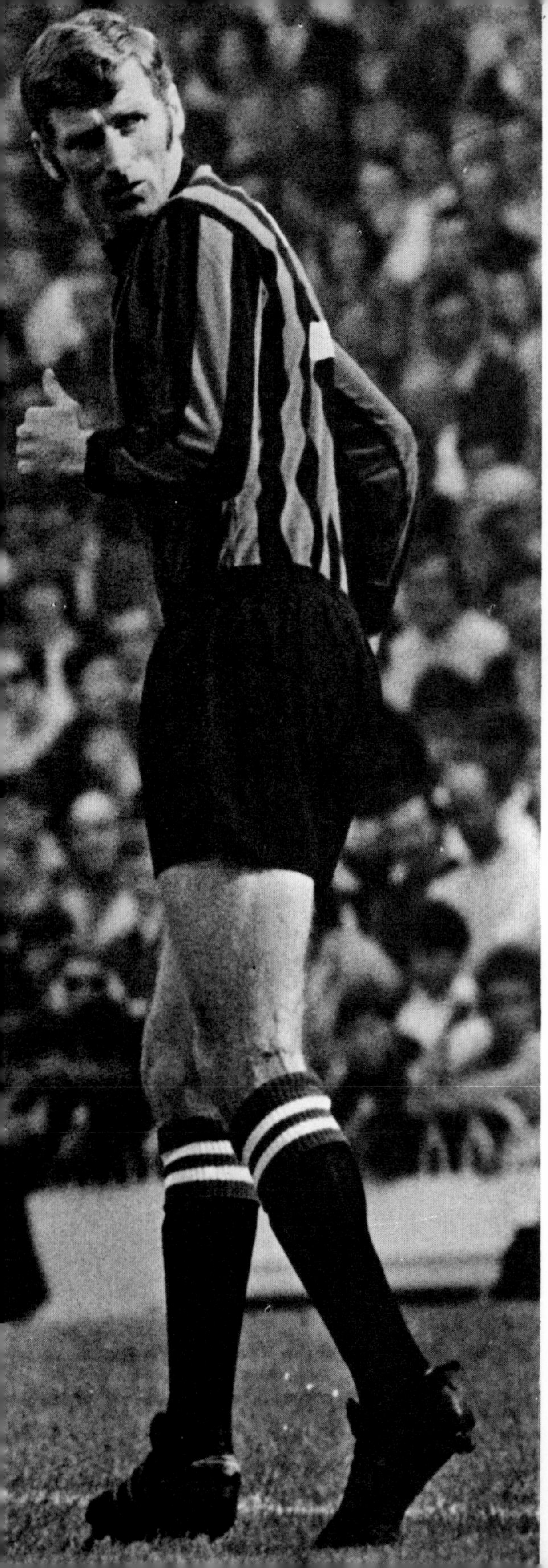

'outfield' for a year or two when they were young I'm sure it would make all the difference.

But if the high ball is being used more and more frequently these days there are other problems for goalkeepers that are not so easy to deal with. Nowadays with so many players packing into the penalty area the goalkeeper's big headache is very often to get a sight of the ball. You've got to be moving about on or near your line *behind* the players, trying to get a look 'round' them to see what's going on, on the ball. Sometimes it's so difficult that a fellow can shoot and you don't even see the ball until it hits the back of the net and there's nothing you can do about that kind of goal.

Commentators and football writers generally don't give enough recognition to this fact of modern football life. Often a goalkeeper is said to be 'lucky' because the ball hits him or maybe he justs gets time to stick out a foot, but to me the important thing is to have your body (or your foot) in the right place and if you do that and stop 'one' you can't call that luck. It's part of the business of keeping goal.

Even so, this isn't the worst thing about the game and the crowded boxes. In the normal way, if you see a player setting himself for a shot, you are on your way as soon as the ball is hit. But with so many players about close to goal, this increases the chance of someone deflecting the ball in flight–even one of your team-mates. On your way to cover the shot, anyone can run across the flight of the ball and get a touch and suddenly you find yourself going the wrong way. All you can do about that is hope that it doesn't crop up too often.

(Left) Manchester City skipper Tony Book, a key figure in the Manchester City success story of recent years. (Right) Keith Weller of Chelsea takes on Book's full back partner at Manchester City, Arthur Mann.

RIGHT BREAKS AND THREE C's ARE ESSENTIAL

says
BOB WILSON

Britain's best
uncapped goalkeeper

Arsenal goalkeeper Bob Wilson, a lively commentator on the game of soccer.

SUMMING up what in my opinion it takes to reach the top class as a goalkeeper–and stay there–I can put it all in six words: three C's and the right breaks. Few other goalkeepers have the personal experiences and frustrations that I have behind me and without bragging I feel that it was because the way up was so long and difficult for me I am better able to appreciate just how important the *breaks* are. I feel sure that few other 'keepers will dispute my three C's as being the basic essentials but there are two kinds of 'break' and having had a bit more than my share of both kinds I really know from hard experience how vitally important they can be.

The three C's are simple: courage, consistency and confidence. Without any one of these three requirements you might as well give up right away but if consistency is a *must* for goalkeepers, courage is an essential ingredient for all players, not just goalkeepers. By courage I don't mean 'cold courage' or bravery. In fact, I get a bit fed up of reading in the newspapers things like . . ."Wilson showed great courage going down at so and so's feet."

Real courage must be a vital, built-in part of every player's game and it shows itself not just in goalkeepers but in all players by the way they go into situations without hesitancy, without losing the tiniest fraction of a second thinking about it. The situation arises–the player reacts immediately–that's what I mean by courage, even if other people do put different interpretations on the word.

The second C–consistency–means bread and butter for goalkeepers. Anyone can go in goal in an emergency, say when the goalkeeper gets injured,

and have an absolute blinder. It's been done often enough to prove the point, but there's all the difference in the world between going between the sticks for the odd half hour or so for ONE game and doing it week in, week out for the whole season.

Of course, all goalkeepers have the odd day when they are a little below par and they even make mistakes but the consistent goalkeeper is the one who can put up his steady, high-standard game during 42 matches, over the whole season. That is consistency and in my opinion the difference between the good goalkeepers, the outstanding few and the great 'keeper.

Once you've hit the top of your game and produced it over a period to become consistent, the third C follows almost automatically. Suddenly you realise that you are an immediate choice for the first team and on top of your form you find yourself humming with confidence. As an individual, I feel that this comes from safe handling and feeling settled in the side. My experience playing for Arsenal after my long and often frustratingly difficult climb to First Division standard has I think made me more aware than most how important this confidence is. Maybe that's why I notice the feeling of the team as a whole–the confidence

Bob Wilson, renowned for his bravery, dives at the feet of West Ham United's Jimmy Greaves to illustrate his technique.

that everyone has at Highbury, in themselves and each other, in our manager and coach Bertie Mee and Don Howe.

Everyone at Arsenal was so aware that this great club had been 17 years without achieving any notable success and having broken this run by winning the Fairs Cup and going on to do consistently well over a long run of games the place simply buzzes with confidence. Out on the park I feel it too, *spreading out* from me in goal. When the goalkeeper is playing well this carries to the other players who see you confident and doing well. I think it seems to them that I can't be beaten.

With that idea in their minds they seem to feel they've got a brick wall built in front of their goal and they push upfield. They'd never do that if they didn't have confidence in the other defenders and in their goalkeeper, but these days Arsenal players press forward every time we win possession of the ball. This supreme confidence is what enables defenders to move up repeatedly; it *spreads* right through the team and as it builds up you begin to think of yourselves (as a team) as *unbeatable*.

But even with the courage, consistency and confidence you still need a bit more than just those three things to make it. You need the right kind of breaks–at the right time–and looking back, without asking for sympathy, I've had plenty of the wrong kind of break and also the right break at the wrong time!

Looking back, I first began to get ideas about being a professional goalkeeper when I played for England schoolboys. It was the same season as Nobby Stiles and Bobby Tambling and, in fact, I was attached as an amateur to Manchester United at the time. It was then, playing for England schoolboys, that I began to think that I was perhaps just that bit better than the average goalkeeper. I thought that I could make it professionally and wanted to join United right away but my father was against it. At the time there was the maximum wage and all that and my father's influence persuaded me to follow up my second love–a general interest in all sports. I was doing pretty well at Grammar School–another of the reasons why my father was against my joining Manchester United–and so I studied and went on to Loughborough College.

I got a lucky break there for the Loughborough team of that year was the best amateur side I've ever seen. We didn't win the FA Amateur Cup for various reasons–one of those things that happen in football, injuries and so on–but we were waltzing through the tournament when we suddenly ran into

Charlie George, a new Arsenal idol at Highbury, has done much to put Arsenal back on the pinnacle of British soccer.

Arsenal full back Pat Rice (left) and Peter Eustace of West Ham make a determined bid to win the ball.

all sorts of injury troubles. It ended for me in the quarter final when I got two broken ribs early in the game and that was a fine example of the wrong type of *break*.

I stayed at Loughborough, completed the course and then did a full year of teaching at a comprehensive school to be a fully qualified teacher, but always at the back of my mind I had this longing to have a go. I didn't know whether I'd make it of course but by this time I was second choice (behind Mike Pinner) for the England Amateur team and during my year as a teacher I had signed for Arsenal as an amateur. Then at the end of the season 1963/64 I got a really big break–six games in Arsenal's first team while still an amateur.

It was great to play in the First Division, but really I wasn't ready for it at the time. But it was a start–the start of a *belated and very long apprenticeship* for me. From then on I had a mixture of hard luck and bad luck–not getting the right breaks–and finally I'm sure that everyone at Highbury had made up their minds that I wasn't going to make it. In the following season, my first as a professional, I got two *breaks* around Christmas 1964 when I was told I was going into the side. I played against Sheffield Wednesday and did quite well, then played again against Fulham on New Year's Day...and broke my arm!

There you can see what I mean about getting the right breaks at the right time. First I went into the league side before I was ready and then the season after I got both kinds of break in the space of a few days. In two games my big opportunity had come and gone and after that I had to wait more than four years for my next chance. Even then, when Jim Furnell was unlucky enough to blot his copy book–he took his eye off the ball in the 89th minute of an FA Cup game against Birmingham, and there was the ball in the back of the net–no one seemed to have any confidence in me.

I took Jim's place for the Cup replay and was then given a more or less guaranteed run for the last 15 or 16 League matches but right through that period everyone was talking about Peter Shilton. You could hardly pick up a newspaper–any paper–without reading something of Arsenal's efforts to sign Shilton and you can imagine how I felt about it. I started late (my own fault) but finally when I did get a

Alan Mullery, skipper of Spurs and a regular choice for England, holds off a challenge from Scotland's Willie Carr, a tigerish young player from Coventry City.

regular run and was nearly 27 years old it seemed that I was only playing out the last few games of the season before going back into the reserves!

I was so frustrated at that time that I applied for a teaching job at Loughborough. I've still got the application forms at home. I felt I was doing well but it seemed to me that my future lay in the reserves. Fortunately the Shilton affair blew over and my form the following season was such that after five or six matches the newspapers said that . . . "Arsenal had called off their search for a goalkeeper".

At the time I felt terrible–the thought that I was being written off as a failure without ever having had a real go, without being given a real chance was what made me so depressed that I was ready to quit.

Now I'm on top of the world with everything going right for me and I want nothing more than to go on playing for Arsenal as long as I can and the way I feel now at 29, I think I could go on for ever. But my big *break* came in the 89th minute–literally the last minute of Jim Furnell's unfortunate Cup game and the 89th minute of my career. I was all for going out of the game when suddenly, right out of the blue, my world turned upside down, and I ended the right way up. But with all this behind me I know just how important it can be for any player to get the right breaks at the right time and the difference between success and failure at a professional level is often slight.

It could be a scene from an ice-dancing pairs championship but in fact Southampton's Jimmy Gabriel finds the shirt of Arsenal's George Armstrong a useful asset in keeping his feet on a snow-covered pitch.

Brian Glanville's
TOP TWENTY

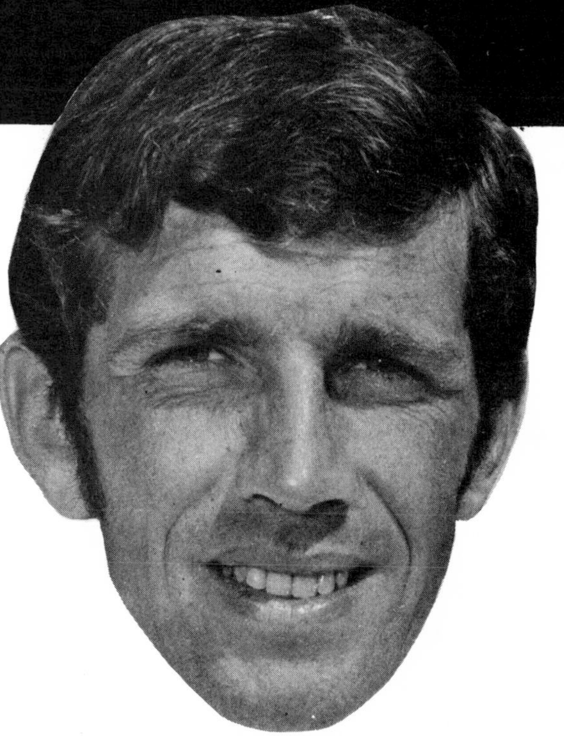

Johnny Giles, the midfield genius of Leeds United.

ATILIO ANCHETA (Nacional and Uruguay) It was obvious when Ancheta, at the age of 21, played at centre-back against England in Montevideo in the summer of 1969 that he was a player to admire. The following year, this large, dark Uruguayan confirmed the impression, when he played a leading role in his team's progress to the semi-finals of the World Cup in Mexico. In the event, they took fourth place, but this was scarcely Ancheta's fault. Moved up into attack after they had bombarded the West German goal for much of the third place match, at the Azteca, he put in a splendid header which produced from Wolter, West Germany's goalkeeper, a still more remarkable one handed save. An excellent technical player, as adept in control as he is at close marking, Ancheta was born on July 19, 1948. He seems to have many World Cups to come.

ROBERT BONINSEGNA (Internazionale and Italy) By an odd irony, it was Boninsegna rather than Riva who was Italy's outstanding striker in the World Cup Final of 1970 against Brazil, Boninsegna who scored the only Italian goal. Pouncing on a careless backheel by Clodoaldo, he raced across the face of the penalty area–and Riva–to put the ball in. The irony lay in the fact that Boninsegna was glad to leave Cagliari for Internazionale, his original club, in 1969, because he was sick of playing second fiddle to Riva, of moving out of the middle to make room for him. Sturdily built, intelligent and brave, Boninsegna was born in Mantua on November 13, 1943. Internazionale spotted him, signed him. But Herrera, then the manager, didn't want him, sold him to Prato, and his League debut was made for Prato in Serie B (the second division) in 1963; he played 22 matches for a single goal. Potenza signed him the following year, when he played 32 matches for nine goals. Next, in his slow climb to the heights, he went at last into Serie A football with Varese, making his debut against, of all teams, Inter, in September, 1965. Cagliari bought him the following season and though he was never a heavy scorer for them, he had a major effect on their attack, winning a League Championship medal in 1969/70. His debut for Italy was made on November 18, 1967 against Switzerland in Berne, after which he promptly lost his place. Inter bought him back in 1970, the goals began to flow faster, but he was only a last minute choice for the World Cup, after Anastasi had dropped out. In Mexico, however, he showed his full, impressive capacity.

TARCISIO BURGNICH (Internazionale and Italy) Right-back. A blue-chinned defender, rather after the style of an Italian Wilf Copping, Burgnich scored a vital and unexpected goal for Italy in the semi-finals of the 1970 World Cup against West Germany but, switched to centre-half, wasn't able to prevent Pelé leaping to head the first goal of the World Cup Final. A dour, combative, hard tackling player of great morale, his career had some odd twists and turns, before he finally settled down with Internazionale, under Herrera, winning Italian Championship, European Cup and Intercontinental Championship medals. He was born on April 25, 1939, at Ruda, in Udine, the north east corner of Italy where so many players come from. Udinese found him, signed him and sold him to Juventus in 1960, the year in which he played for the Italian Olympic team in the football tournament. Burgnich, who made his Serie A debut for Udinese on June 2, 1959, when Milan beat them 7–0, didn't settle with Juventus. After one season and only 13 games, he went to Palermo, played 31, and was promptly bought by Inter. He played twice in the 1966 World Cup–though not in the traumatic defeat by North Korea–and was one of the most admired players in their 1970, Mexican, side.

HECTOR CHUMPITAZ (Universitario and Peru) One of the most engaging players of the 1970 World Cup, Chumpitaz frequently alarmed his team manager, then the Brazilian, Didi, with his storming excursions out of defence. Though he is not tall, he is sturdily and powerfully built. He hits long passes out of defence with great facility and force, and his free kicks, taken right footed, are notable. The most memorable of all, in Mexico, was the one which tore past the Bulgarian goalkeeper to score in an eliminating match. Chumpitaz also climbs great heights to the ball, compensating for his lack of inches. A star of the team which knocked out Argentina in their South American qualifying group, Chumpitaz did not miss a game in the 1970 Finals, when Peru were eliminated in the quarter-finals by Brazil.

CLODOALDO (Santos and Brazil) A right-half who, despite a silly back-heel which cost Brazil a goal in the Final, emerged as one of the most exciting young stars of the 1970 World Cup. In the early games, the 20 year old Santos half-back played a somewhat restrained game, as though he were under instructions–and slightly overawed by his distinguished elders. But as the competition advanced, so he shed his inhibitions, started coming forward, deploying his skills on the ball, his intelligent use of it, and his ability to go forward and score–as he did in the quarter-finals against Peru. Santos are his only major club. He made his debut for them at the age of 17, his debut for Brazil against England at the Maracana in Rio in 1969. Injury thereafter set back his international career, but the World Cup resoundingly confirmed it.

Tarcisio Burgnich, full back for Italy.

Teofilo Cubillas, an outstanding player from Peru.

TEOFILO CUBILLAS (Alianza and Peru) The electric dribbling, the cool, effective finishing of the little, coloured Peruvian inside-forward, Cubillas, made him an outstanding figure in the 1970 World Cup; and at the early age of 20. He gave warning of his potential in the opening game, against Bulgaria, when he scored the winning goal with a strong, right footed shot, after a typically elusive run. He proceeded to get Peru's only goal against West Germany, with a shot which was deflected, another couple against Morocco, and one more against Brazil, in the quarter finals, making him one of the most dangerous and prolific strikers in the tournament. He had previously scored the first of Peru's three goals against Bolivia in August 1969, in the qualifying competition, but he arrived in Mexico largely unknown to the world at large.

JOHNNY GILES (Leeds United and Eire) Johnny Giles is one of the great, unappreciated architects of Leeds United's recent success; unappreciated, that is to say, beyond Elland Road. He has always tended to do good by stealth: his ideal is to be in the right place at the right time to help a colleague, whether it be in defence or in attack. His free kicks are always beautifully flighted, his penalties placed with cool aplomb. Joining Manchester United as a boy, he was always an inside-forward by inclination, but sometimes a winger by necessity. It was on the right wing that he won a Cup medal with United in 1963, but as an inside-forward that he played against Spurs in the semi-finals of 1962, and felt himself unfairly blamed for United's defeat. This had something to do with his quarrel with the club when he was dropped after a Charity Shield defeat, in 1963, and his transfer to Leeds United. There he played at first as a right winger, but he had been bought as an eventual replacement to the team's Scottish general, Bobby Collins, who he much admired: when Collins went, Giles stepped into his place with immediate success. His link-up with Bremner in midfield is outstanding, his absence always a great handicap to the team. Many times capped for Eire and once, at least, rather petulantly dropped by them, he would doubtless have had far more kudos had he played for a more "fashionable" international team. As it is, he has helped Leeds to success in the champion-

ship, the Fairs Cup and the Football League Cup; which will do to be going on with.

JURGEN GRABOWSKI (Eintracht Frankfurt and West Germany) The curious thing about Grabowski's success in the 1970 World Cup, when he turned the English defence inside out as a second half substitute in Leon, is that he was discarded by West Germany just before the 1966 competition. It took him over four years to re-establish himself in an international team for which he had made his debut in May, 1966 against Eire in Dublin. Germany won 4–0 and Grabowski, keeping his place at outside-right for the next game, three days later, against Northern Ireland in Belfast, might have been expected to have a run in the World Cup. Instead, after playing again against Rumania in Ludwigshafen and finishing on a winning German side for the third successive occasion, he was discarded, and did not play again until the following October, against the Turks, in Ankara; another victory, after which he was promptly dropped, again. So he was a rather controversial and unexpected choice for Mexico, but this quick adventurous winger, with fine ball control, acceleration and an excellent centre, would turn out to be a trump card. Helmut Schoen, his team manager, had evidently decided from the first to use him as a dangerous substitute. He came on for Helmut Haller in the first match, against Morocco, for Lohr against Bulgaria, Libuda against Peru. Against England, he replaced Libuda, overwhelmed an exhausted Terry Cooper, and transformed the game. His reward was to play the whole of the semi-final against Italy, though he did not appear in the third place match against Uruguay. It was in no small measure thanks to him that West Germany had got there.

FRANZ HASIL (Feyenoord and Austria) A major figure in the 1970 European Cup Final in Milan, when his tremendous shooting, energy and enterprise were a feature of the match, Franz Hasil is an Austrian international who has reached his full stature in Holland. He was brought to Rotterdam in 1969 by his fellow Austrian Ernst Happel, the Dutch club's manager, who had known him since he was a veteran defender and Hasil a pro-

Steve Heighway, a Liverpool discovery and one of the sensations of the 1971 season in England.

mising junior with Rapid Vienna. At first Hasil impressed nobody in Rotterdam; he was felt to be all skill and no sense, besides seeming unfit. He had arrived from the Bundesliga club Schalke 04, who had brought him to West Germany the previous year. But Hasil did not get on well with the Schalke 04 manager, Rudi Gutendorf, and Happel brought him to Feyenoord. By this time he was an Austrian international and, up to the end of the season in which Feyenoord won the European Cup, had been capped thirteen times. He is essentially a midfield player, with a talent for suddenly going forward and hitting tremendous, right footed shots. He played a great part in Feyenoord's unexpected victory in the European Cup. Born July 28, 1944.

STEVE HEIGHWAY (Liverpool and Eire) Luckily for the Republic of Ireland, Steve Heighway agreed to play for Eire when he was chosen, against Poland, early in season 1970/71. This may have had something to do with his remarkable swift rise to fame. He had only just, at the age of 22, turned professional with Liverpool, and he had yet to play a full League match for them. Within a matter of weeks, this lean, incisive player had become one of the most dangerous centre-forwards in the League, sure of a place in a Liverpool attack in which £100,000 players could find themselves discarded. For a footballer who, only a season earlier, had been playing for Skelmersdale in Northern amateur football, the transition was little short of incredible. Heighway's tremendous acceleration, his willingness to go it alone, his strong finishing, made him not only a new star, but the living refutation of the idea that successful pros must begin as 15 year olds. All the more ironic that Coventry City then, when he was studying economics for a B.Sc. degree at Warwick, should let him elude their grasp. So Liverpool got him for nothing.

DAVID HAY (Celtic and Scotland) A revelation of the 1969/70 season, the blond David Hay established himself in Celtic's team, marching towards the European Cup Final, as a fine, attacking right-back, though he ended it as a midfield player for Scotland, in the home international tournament. In this role, though he did what he honestly could, a lack of acceleration blunted his edge, but some of his overlapping for Celtic, not least in the European semi-finals against Leeds, was exhilarating. In the Final,

Ladislav Petras, who emerged during the Mexico World Cup finals as a player of the highest class. Petras is one of this year's International Football Book contributors.

Jurgen Grabowski, a skilful winger who did much to boost West Germany's aspirations in Mexico last year.

he played in the team disappointingly beaten in Milan by Feyenoord, but he had consolation in the shape of a League Championship medal, won for playing 25 games in Celtic's triumphant season; his first as a regular member of the side.

RINUS ISRAEL (Feyenoord and Holland) The wonderfully versatile performance of Rinus Israel, captain, sweeper, stopper and goal scorer, had much to do with Feyenoord beating Celtic in the 1970 European Cup Final. He began the game as sweeper, a quick and very perceptive one, but after Celtic had taken the lead, he stole upfield to a free kick and, when the ball was headed across to him, nodded it in for the equaliser. In the second half, with Feyenoord now on top, Israel moved into his more familiar position in the back four, releasing one of the two stoppers to play in midfield. Born in Amsterdam on March 19, 1942, he began his first class career as a part-timer with the local DWS club, in 1962. In due course he gave up his job as a building worker (laying pavements) and in 1966, he joined Feyenoord for about £30,000. Outside the game, he owns a cigar shop in Rotterdam. By the end of 1970, he had won 35 Dutch international caps.

GEORGES LECH (Sochaux and France) When France beat an Argentinian XI 4–3 in Buenos Aires early in 1971, a most unexpected result, the star of the French team was its busy inside-right Georges Lech, who quickly made the first goal, and later scored one on his own account. Lech was praised by the Argentinian critics, one of whom said that with his skill and flair, he could hold a place in any international team in the world. It was a most pleasing affirmation for a player who, after a brilliant and precocious beginning, seemed to have lost ground. After his triumph at the Boca Juniors stadium, Lech remarked how pleasant it was now to play in the French national team; no longer was there the depressing atmosphere he experienced when he came into the side as a teenager, ill at ease among the veterans. This was as long ago as October, 1963, when he played outside-right against Bulgaria in Paris in a Nations Cup qualifying match, went on to win a string of caps on the wings, but had lost his place by the time the 1966 World Cup came round. He was then with Lens, where he made his name but left, in due course, after bitter disputes;

whereupon the club sacked his father, who was employed at the stadium. It's significant that even at the time of his first caps, an annual should describe him as "a winger, but with all the qualities of an inside-forward". These, now he has settled happily with Sochaux, he has displayed to the full. He was born at Montigny-en-Goelle on June 2, 1945, and his brother, Bernard, is also a professional footballer.

ALAN MULLERY (Tottenham Hotspur and England) Born in North Kensington, Alan Mullery joined Fulham from school, and cost the Spurs £72,500 when he joined them early in 1964. He was a regular member of the Fulham First Division team at the age of eighteen, eager and combative, hitting those long through balls in which he still rejoices. His international career, till it came to full fruition in the World Cup of 1970 in Mexico, had been rather an odd one. Thus, he missed England's 1964 tour of the Americas because he ricked his back while shaving. He then got capped against Holland, the following season, but subsequently lost his place, till injuries to Nobby Stiles in season 1966/7 let him back again. Mullery seized his chance and stayed there, improving beyond all expectation. He continued to keep Stiles out of the side in Mexico, and repeated the fine performance he had given against Pelé in Rio, the previous year. But he will be remembered in that tournament above all for his marvellous goal against West Germany in the quarter finals at Leon, a goal he not only scored but engineered, beginning the England movement, then sending Newton down the wing with a fine crossfield pass, before dashing into position, across the pitch, to convert his centre on the near post. He has been criticised for lack of pace, but his all round qualities, his morale, his combativity, have forged him into a player of undoubted international quality.

VLADIMIR MUNTIJAN (Dynamo Kiev and Russia) One of the best and technically most accomplished Russian players in the World Cup, Vladimir Muntijan, at the age of 23, clearly had a substantial future. He began to play football at the age of 11, was intended to become an acrobat, but fell ill with chest trouble and went to hospital for four months. His family moved on his account, his new friends played football; and so did he. He went to a sports school in Kiev, represented the city, then the Ukraine, at schoolboy level, as an inside-left, then in 1963 he naturally joined Kiev Dynamo. Small for his age, nobody noticed him much, at first, but in 1965, at the age of 19, he won his way into the first team. He was one of the young Kiev team which won the title in 1966 in the absence of many first teamers, called up by the World Cup side, who then found themselves unable to regain their place. He pays great tribute to the coaching of Mikhail Korsounski at his sports school, and to the Kiev manager, Viktor Maslov. A midfield player now, his concept of the role is that it should be 70% attack and 30% defence, he himself believing, quite correctly, that his chief gifts are those of an attacker. By the time the 1970 World Cup arrived, he'd won ten caps, to which he added four more, in Mexico. He intends to teach physical education.

Rivelino, the superbly talented Brazilian with a devastating body-swerve and a dynamic shot.

LADISLAV PETRAS (Inter Bratislava and

Czechoslovakia) The Czechs had little to be pleased about in the World Cup of 1970, but one cause for faint consolation was the splendid form of their blond striker, Petras. Largely unknown before the competition, he made the best and quickest possible impact with a fine goal in their opening match in Guadalajara, to put them ahead against Brazil. It was a characteristic one; the fruit of power, acceleration and the courage to go through alone. After he had scored it, Petras knelt crossing himself; and he might, soon afterwards, have scored again. 23 years old at the time, he had come into the Czech national side only the previous December, helping them to their surprising 4–1 play off victory against the Hungarians, in Marseilles, and thus to a place in Mexico. The game, however, finished on a rather unhappy note for Petras himself, for he was sent off, five minutes from the end. Originally a left winger with Banska Bystrica, he helped them up to the First Division, scored 20 goals for them, making him top scorer in the Championship, but failed to save them from relegation. Inter Bratislava then signed him. After the World Cup, he was suspended, along with all the other Czech players, from international football, after alleged irregularities over the wearing of branded football boots.

Alan Mullery, who has made enormous strides during the past 12 months.

ROBERTO RIVELINO (Corinthians Sao Paolo and Brazil) It was a typical, ferocious, swerving, left footed free kick by Rivelino which equalised for Brazil against Czechoslovakia in their opening World Cup match in Guadalajara. The powerfully made, heavily sideburned and moustached Rivelino went on to score two more goals in the competition, and to make the first goal of the World Cup Final for Pelé, with a high, accurate left wing centre. His left footed shooting rivalled that of Puskas–and of Gerson, for so long his rival and, in the 1970 team, his colleague. For both are essentially midfield players, formidable left footers, suspect in their stamina. Rivelino won a place in Brazil's 1968 touring side in Europe, at the expense of Gerson, went on later that year to play, and score, against the Rest of the World, in Rio, but still could not establish himself in the team. Zagalo found the answer when he picked both men, deploying Rivelino as a nominal left winger, operating chiefly in midfield; but coming up to shoot, and score. An excellent ball player, the 24 year old Rivelino complemented Gerson, instead of duplicating him. They each played a large part in Brazil's success.

WIM VAN HANEGEM (Feyenoord and Holland) An excellent performance in the European Cup Final against Celtic in Milan, in May, 1970, put the seal on a marvellous season for the 25 year old Van Hanegem. Tall and well built, the possessor of a marvellous left foot, he had headed one of the goals whereby his club, in an earlier round, put out the holders, Milan. That November evening, he was the best player on the field. He joined Feyenoord only in 1969, after his former club, the famous Xerces of Rotterdam, had had to drop out of the League. Before that, he had played for a team called Velox. His success with Feyenoord won him a place in the Dutch national side, too. Though he can score goals, and likes to go into the goal area, his role is that of a midfield player, and in the European Final, against Celtic, he largely lay deep, making fine use of his left footed passing.

SILVANO VILLA (Milan) A new and sudden discovery of the 1970/71 season, the 19 year old

Villa won a regular place in Milan's fine attack, despite the challenge of famous, much more experienced, players. It was a remarkable step from Third Division, Serie C, football with Alessandria, to whom he had been lent the previous season. Confidence, however, is the keynote of his game. He was not even demoralised when he broke a leg, playing for Milan's reserve team and, as a more or less direct consequence, found himself packed off to Alessandria. His resilience may have something to do with his parentage and the circumstances of their meeting. His father, a soft drinks seller, is Italian, but his mother is Russian, and they met during the war in a Nazi concentration camp, at Leipzig. Villa himself was born on August 13, 1951, played for a junior club called Villasanta, was coveted by the nearby Monza club, but brought to Milan by one of their fans. As a centre-forward, he is brave, dashing, and enterprising. He made his debut at San Siro when he came on as a substitute against Varese on September 2, 1970, and promptly scored a spectacular headed goal.

BERTI VOGTS (Borussia Munchengladbach and West Germany) One of the best all round full-backs in the world, a fine defender and an excellent, overlapping attacker, Vogts was a member of the West German side which took third place in the 1970 World Cup. Earlier in the year, he had helped his club win the Championship of the Bundesliga, and he competed in the European Cup, the following season. Blond and stockily made, admirably balanced, he joined Borussia in 1965 from VfR Buttgen as an eighteen year old, and by the time he reached Mexico, where he played at right-back in all but the third place game, when he switched to the left, he had already played in 23 internationals. Oddly enough, his debut was made as a left-back, in tandem with the very player who was at right-back in the third place match against Uruguay, Patzke. The occasion was a surprising 1–0 defeat by Rumania in Bucharest on November 22, 1967. Dropped from the ensuing game against Albania, Vogts returned, at right-back, to play against Belgium in Brussels the following March, and has been a regular international player ever since.

Berti Vogts, accomplished full back from West Germany.

THE HARD WAY TO THE TOP BUT IT WAS WORTH IT

by JAIRZINHO

Brazil's outstanding winger in Mexico

After I returned from Mexico City to Rio de Janeiro with my colleagues and the World Cup I was asked often why I'd run off the pitch against Uruguay and gone down on my knees to pray. I've always been brought up to be religious, though I've never prayed that I should score goals or win matches and things like that. But at big moments, at critical times in my life, I find it the most natural thing to do . . . just sit and pray.

Other players might take things for granted but I never could–right from an early age life was difficult for me as it is for millions of other youngsters in South America and when I scored goals in the big World Cup games I found I spontaneously wanted to pray, to thank God that things had worked out for me and I'd been lucky enough to contribute something to help my team. I'd wanted to do it before, during the World Cup in Mexico, but after the Czech player Ladislav Petras had done it–when he scored a great goal against us in our opening game–I felt I had to keep a tighter hold on myself and control my emotions.

But when I got that goal in the semi-final against Uruguay–we'd been losing 1-0 at half time–I just couldn't control myself. Against all my attempts at self-discipline, there I was running off the pitch and

Italian goalkeeper Albertosi lies prostrate at the feet of Jairzinho in Mexico with Italy's skipper Facchetti looking on.

throwing myself down on the grass to kneel and pray. Why? Because just at that moment, with the ball in the Uruguayan net, I happened to remember that nine months earlier I had sustained a serious injury and even after an operation it looked unlikely that I would get the chance even to play in the World Cup.

The injury I received in 1969 was a serious one, necessitating a bone graft that didn't *take* the first time. The bone in my left foot just wouldn't mend and at one time the doctors said I was finished. I couldn't play any more!

Then the surgeons tried again and finally, wearing a specially made football boot with an extra stud just where I needed it, I gradually returned to fitness. But during my inactivity I'd obviously lost my place in the national team. In addition, Rogerio and Roberto, right winger and centre forward for my club Botafogo, had played so well it seemed I was set for a long spell of reserve team duty.

Fortunately things worked out, my injury cleared up completely; except that the extra stud gives me a corn on the sole of my foot and is often rather painful. But after all I'd been through that's nothing when balanced against the joy of helping to win the Copa Jules Rimet for Brazil and keep it in Rio for all time.

I said earlier that my life has been a hard and difficult one but judge for yourself. I was born in a town called Caxias near Rio de Janeiro and when I was two years old my father died. My mother had to work as a servant until I was 19. Then I was able to take care of her but for those 17 years in between I lived in Rio with an aunt.

My mother sent money to my aunt for my food and as well as having to pay my school fees she also managed to send me a little pocket money too–but never enough to buy a pair of football boots. Until I was 15 years old my football was played in the street, barefooted like everyone else, but at that age I left school and got a trial with Flamengo, a First

Division club in Rio.

I also got a job as a typist where the boss was a Director of the Flamengo club, but I couldn't always get away from work to train when Flamengo wanted me and they turned me down. At about the same time I was also sacked from my job and then for some time I worked as a clerk for a car company.

My first football club was called *Brasileirinho* (little Brazil) and our barefoot championship was played in street games. I was seven years old at the time and after my early years playing barefoot I had a terrible time when I finally played in a well organised amateur club and was given and forced to wear football boots. They were so strange and uncomfortable I could hardly move and couldn't kick the ball more than 10 yards without hurting my feet.

Later, after my failure with Flamengo, I joined another amateur team called Torres Homens and playing for them against Botafogo's juniors I did rather well and their junior coach, Paraguaio (he is a fine man doing a great job for the club and still there now with the youngsters), asked me if I would like a trial.

Of course I accepted and apparently did well. I remember I scored a goal that day and for the next six months I trained with the club. Then in 1961, when I was 16, I signed for them and in my first three seasons played in the youth team that won the Rio Junior championship, playing on the wing and at centre forward.

In 1963 I got my first big chance and was chosen to play for Brazil in the Pan-American Games. The competition was staged that year in Sao Paulo, Brazil, and it was in these matches that I first played with Carlos Alberto (our World Cup captain in Mexico) and my Botafogo club-mate Roberto. We won the championship with an all-amateur team and within a few weeks I got my first chance to play in the Botafogo senior team.

Looking back I have no doubt at all how lucky I was to have joined a club like Botafogo. My debut was in an away game against the Millonarios club of Bogota, Colombia, in the Libertadores Cup (our South American equivalent of the European Cup). "Lucky" because Botafogo were representing Brazil in this big tournament and lucky also to find myself playing in really exalted company. I'd had no chance to train with the first team squad previously but the other players were really great with Didi, Nilton Santos, Zagalo and Gerson amongst them.

Of course, they are all better known than I am– the first three helping Brazil win the World Cup in 1958 and 1962 while Gerson was one of our biggest stars in Mexico and Zagalo was there again–as the team manager. He was also the Botafogo boss at the time of our success in Mexico. With players like them around you, any youngster would be both proud and

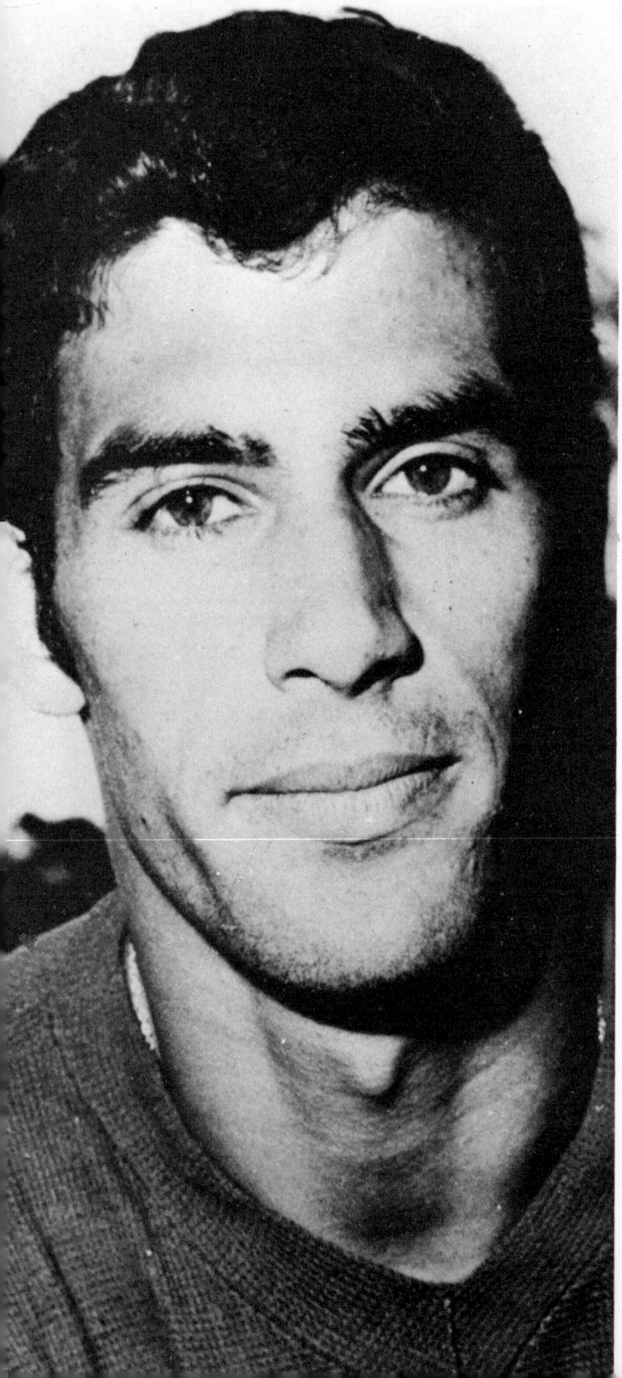

Atilio Ancheta, an accomplished international from Uruguay.

nervous (as I most certainly was) but though they made things easy for me I must confess that I didn't play very well.

At that time Botafogo had one other great star, Garrincha, and he was the man that I stood in for while he was unfit, against Millonarios. I couldn't expect to keep my place–it wasn't *my* place as everyone knew for Garrincha was an automatic choice and a great star. Everything he did was sheer magic and he was always my particular idol.

Training with him and watching him in action I learned an awful lot but I realised very quickly that I could never hope to replace him or ever become half the player he was, no matter how I tried. Garrincha was a genius, and everything he did was sensational. But if I knew I didn't have the talent he had I could and did learn a great deal from him–from him especially but also from training and playing with Didi, Zagalo, Gerson, Nilton Santos and later, of course (with Brazil), the fabulous Pele.

Even this chance in Botafogo's team was only the beginning of my way up for I was a right winger and I spent the next six years as reserve to Garrincha and it was only when he was injured that I got a chance to play in what I feel is my best position on the right wing. But the Botafogo club tried me at centre forward and it was in the middle that I established myself and finally became a regular member of the Brazilian national team.

After the Mexico World Cup I have played 66 international games for Brazil, some on the right wing but mostly at centre forward, and in these

Burnley goalkeeper Tony Waiters provides an unwilling 'seat' for Tottenham forward Jimmy Pearce.

Crystal Palace goalkeeper John Jackson saves brilliantly a shot from a Leeds United forward during a match at Selhurst Park.

matches I have scored 28 goals. But none sweeter or more precious to me than the one I was lucky enough to get against Uruguay in the 1970 World Cup semi final!

Our success in Mexico came as a big surprise to many Europeans but how could they know that the CBD and Zagalo, our tecnico, were preparing more intensively for the World Cup than ever before. Really they thought of everything. It started with the complete squad getting what I think is best described as a complete physical "brainwash".

While the European teams were still playing league games in their own countries we were locked away in a Brazilian convent and being licked into superb physical shape. After that we moved our HQ to Guanajuato in Mexico where we spent the most decisive 21 days of our physical preparations toning up the basic fitness we'd already attained and adapting it to suit the Mexican conditions.

This, and Zagalo's enormous contribution–his training methods–stopping and starting training matches to explain (right at the time) the things he wanted and did not want. These I think were the secrets of Brazil's success.

On the other side it must be admitted that I believe our opponents made a great many errors. While we lived out in the "Wilds" at Guanajuato, completely isolated from the rest of the world, our opponents were "living" right in the centre of things.

At Guanajuato, where we continued to live the modest, spartan-type existence we had settled into in that convent back in Brazil, the England players were staying at the Guadalajara Hilton Hotel–the centre of the glossy night life of the city, surrounded by beautiful women, bars and night clubs. The Czechs were living in another paradise–the Malibu Hotel–with the players always in the sun or the hotel swimming pool, sharing it with pretty girls.

Meanwhile we Brazilians were kept almost exclusively out of the limelight. Even the journalists and photographers were permitted only a maximum of one hour each day "inside" the artificial wall built around us by the CBD. This was designed to keep out the tourists, the distractions . . . and maybe the inevitable.

We lived like monks in our seclusion and I'll give just one precise example of the different attitudes. We Brazilians, spending all our lives in the tropics, were accustomed to the heat, the sun, but we were afraid of it! While our opponents swam and relaxed, sun-bathing–we actually were hiding from it. I remember one occasion when Wilson Piazza dived in "our" pool and Pelé immediately called to him to come out. "The sun is too hot," he told Piazza.

I don't say this to suggest that our opponents behaved irregularly or were not professional in their attitude. But many people are easily influenced (Brazilians included) and while our rivals were exposed to all the attractions Guadalajara has to offer, we were hidden from them.

Zagalo made more important contributions to Brazil's success, particularly in the field of violence and retaliation. Personally, since the injury that threatened my career, I have always been a little edgy and intolerant of opponents who kick. But I remember during a training game against a Mexican team when Rivelino was being kicked all over the place and retaliated, Zagalo ran on to the pitch. He told Rivelino that this was a very serious thing. That in Mexico we must expect kicking and never, *never* retaliate in case someone should get sent off. It was a real lesson for us all, this rebuke for Rivelino, and it made a big impression on me.

Later in our semi-final with Uruguay, my opponent Mujica got in three really good kicks at me in the first five minutes. I even surprised myself by the way I took this treatment and I remember telling him quite calmly . . . "go on, kick all you like. It won't make any difference to the result because we are still going to score six goals against you."

In the end we only got four–after a real rocket from Zagalo at half time–the only occasion when I knew him to be angry with us. He insisted that we play our football instead of allowing Uruguay to dictate to us and control a rough game. It did the trick too–Clodoaldo's goal (the equaliser) and the genius of Pelé and finally *we danced our samba round them* to rub out the memory of that World Cup final match of 1950 when Uruguay beat Brazil 2–1.

Lastly a word about some of the best players we faced in Mexico. Banks, of course, is the best goalkeeper in the world and I thought the best defenders were Dobias (Czechoslovakia), Schesternev (USSR), Moore (England). Moore is a great player. His anticipation is fantastic and he was the chief organiser in the English defence always in the right place. But the only English player with what I call real flair and imagination was Bobby Charlton.

In midfield Beckenbauer and Overath (West Germany) were splendid players and so, too, were Italy's Mazzola and Domenghini while in attack I liked the German trio Muller, Seeler and Libuda; Lee (England), Riva (Italy), Dumitrache (Rumania) and Cubillas (Uruguay).

But above all, perhaps, Czechoslovakia's Petras who scored that great goal against us, but he in my opinion is more like a South American player than a European.

Mike Doyle (4) of Manchester City and Tottenham Hotspur's Martin Peters jump for a high ball but it eludes both of them.

'Strong-man' Alan Ball seems to be providing Brian Labone (right) and Ron Davies with extra support during a Wales-England international.

Czech's World Cup failure difficult to explain

by LADISLAV PETRAS

(Czechoslovakia)

Ladislav Petras says there was no lack of endeavour on the part of the Czechoslovakian players during the Mexico World Cup finals.

Although his name may not be familiar, Ladislav Petras was the one Czech player to show up well in the highest company in Mexico. An unknown 23-year-old and first capped only a few months earlier, everyone who saw his spectacular opening goal against Brazil will never forget it–or the obvious pleasure the thrill of scoring gave him. With the ball in the net and the Czechs unexpectedly one up against Brazil, the big favourites, after only 11 minutes, there was a delighted Petras down on his knees 'crossing' himself as if to say ... 'one more please'. He got another–after only four minutes in the game against Rumania, but it wasn't enough. They were the only goals the Czechs scored in Mexico and they lost all three games they played.

MANY people have asked me to explain the disappointing performance of the Czech team in the 1970 World Cup, and though I don't really feel competent to explain exactly why, I have had to try. One thing I do know is that there were in circulation, irresponsible tales of "players playing cards while others were training" and more rumours of the squad splitting up into cliques.

Certainly that was rubbish, although, of course, while there was a good team-spirit throughout the squad it is inevitable that one or two players have particular friends and tend to spend their free moments together. In my case, for example, I am particularly friendly with Ladislav Kuna and Josef Adamec who play for Spartak Trnava and Karel Jokl who plays for our Bratislava neighbours Slovan. Back home we are all less than half an hour away from each other by car and we are all good friends–why shouldn't we be together in Mexico and why does this necessarily have to be a 'clique' within the squad?

Another thing I am sure of is that everyone gave of his best. How can you pull your country's shirt over your head, knowing that the whole world is watching and outside there are 75,000 people and players like Pele, Jairzinho and Rivelino waiting for you without being keyed up?

It's ridiculous to suggest that our failure was due to complacency or lack of effort. Though I'm not a coach or a psychologist, my opinion, for what it's worth, is that we had a hard time playing three games a week to finish the home championship before we left for Mexico and we were probably unable to recover physically for the challenge that the Mexican conditions presented in the short time available.

Whatever the fans or spectators might think, they can get excited and be mentally tired at the end of a match, but I try hard not to get dejected when we are losing and in a similar way I don't get excited when we are ahead and think it's easy. To be honest, I don't think very much at all while the game is going on–you are too involved as a player–and though I have a reputation at home for being 'brave in the enemy penalty area' I'm not aware of it at all.

If there is any substance in this kind of thing, I think it's an *instinct* for scoring chances that takes a player into a certain position and I've come to this conclusion more from watching other players rather than any analysis of my own game. At the final whistle, whether we've won or lost, I'm too tired to think–just physically exhausted–sometimes too tired even to have any feelings of elation or disappointment and I don't think I'm much different from other players in this respect.

Many people tend to sub-divide the football world into categories and argue about whether the British style is best or whether the Brazilians are superior, but I like and admire both styles. The Brazilians obviously have tre-

Ladislav Petras scores a goal that made him famous. It was the Czech's first goal against Brazil in Guadalajara.

Everton's Joe Royle takes on Derby County centre half Roy McFarland. Both these fine young players won their initial England caps against Malta.

mendous skill with the ball but the English are quicker and in my opinion no other country can copy either of them. Learn from them, yes, but try and copy would be disastrous.

It's difficult enough–really hard work–to become a good player in your own right, playing your natural game, but it would be practically impossible to do this and then try to play the 'Brazilian' or 'English' way.

To give another illustration of the gap that separates the spectators from the players I have often been asked how many games I've played or how many goals I've scored. I really just don't know–you just play and play and take each game, and every goal, as it comes without thinking about it or keeping scores–yet those that ask such questions are usually surprised when you say you don't know.

Of course, some things stick in your mind more than others and for me so far there have been two high spots. The first was my debut for Czechoslovakia against Hungary in Marseille at the end of 1969. We had tied on points in our qualifying group but I hadn't played in any of those games. We beat Hungary 4–1 in the play off and though I didn't score myself it was a real thrill for me personally. Anyone who tries to pretend that players don't care ...they said it at home about us after Mexico...should have seen and shared the delight of everyone after we had beaten the Hungarians and qualified.

The other big moment for me was the goal I got against Brazil in the World Cup proper. There was about ten minutes gone and no score and we had been attacking but the move broke down. Carlos Alberto had the ball about ten or fifteen yards away and I sprinted over to have a go at him and won the ball, looked up and set off towards goal. Again I have to say it–you don't think at moments like that–for one thing there's no time for football's not like chess. I just hit the ball at the moment I *felt* it was right–and we were winning!

I know some players tend to worry before big games or be anxious about certain opponents but for me they are all the same. I just take each game as it comes and if I can honestly say that I prefer a good, sporting game I'm not bothered about it if the play becomes a little rough. I said before that I'm 'supposed' to be brave in the box but bravery or whatever you call it isn't everything even against rough defenders.

In my opinion the most important thing is how the ball is played to you, for there's all the difference between a ball that's kicked at you and a good pass that's delivered just right . . . exactly where you want it. If you are closely marked by an opponent this

Derek Dougan of Wolverhampton Wanderers leaps over Chelsea goalkeeper Peter Bonetti.

makes all the difference and I like the kind of ball that's given in such a way that I can take it *on the run with my feet*.

At the same time it's also vitally important that the ball arrives on the opposite side of me from the man marking me–that is if I am running with the defender on my right I like to find the ball running up alongside me on my left hand side. If someone is just going to 'kick' the ball at you and hope, they might as well send you a hand grenade as a football . . . for all too often the result is the same.

For the future I have all kinds of ambitions and although I have a good job as a trained locksmith I'd like to stay in football as long as I can. Of course I'd like to improve my game–to be half as good as Pele would be quite something, though I know I'll never do that for he is the king . . . perfection in everything he does.

But more than improving, survival is important as I have already learned from the experiences of colleagues. A broken leg jeopardised the career of my Inter colleague Juraj Szikora (what a fine player) and of course being a Czech I cannot forget the fate of Rudolf Kucera who played for Dukla. In the 1960's he seemed almost certain to become one of the world's outstanding players. He had everything, really he had it all, but a head injury when he was little more than twenty years old put him out of the game for good.

Off the field and away from football I like driving and music–Johnny Cash and Slovak Folk Songs, many of which have been modernised are my favourites. And being a Slovak I like to eat too, specially our Vepro-knedlo-Zelo and Pivo . . . roast pork, dumplings and sauerkraut with beer . . . and Czech beer is the best in the world!

But football has opened the door to a new world and a new life for me and I want to go on playing. I've got some good memories already, and a shirt I exchanged with Brazil's Carlos Alberto that I prize more highly than anything and wouldn't sell at any price. But most of all–and I'm sure this is true of all my colleagues who played in the 1970 World Cup–I'd love another chance . . . the opportunity to show everyone that the disappointing performance of the Czech team in Mexico was not truly representative of us or our game. And I hope that chance will come in 1974.

The Newcastle United defence can do little as Alan Birchenall (third from the left) scores a tremendous goal for Crystal Palace.

£100 a week referees will not improve the game or its image

says TERRY HENNESSEY
(Wales and Derby County)

SOME people in and around the game appear to believe that the introduction of full-time referees, earning £100 a week, would do for refereeing what the removal of the maximum wage clause did for the game itself. But, personally, even if referees could, and perhaps should, receive a little more financial reward I don't believe it would make any great difference.

Every referee, surely, wants to be known as a good whistler, just as players want to be known and respected for their ability. Each referee has his pride and a desire to be respected. He wants to be fit and to keep up with the play and they must all recognise that the only way they can earn the respect they want is to handle each game the best way they know how.

With thousands of people watching, referees obviously don't want trouble but it seems to me that while the whole of society is going through a difficult period, football is being subjected to the wrong kind of publicity. We have had irresponsible behaviour for years but a few hooligans getting into trouble before or after a match gets the game a bad name. People just blame it all on football, on the game itself, and if a player or players misbehave during a game it seems to be accepted that this must inevitably have a reaction amongst the crowd.

Obviously the referee has got a very difficult job and it's something I would hate to do. They make mistakes, of course, but I'm sure they really are genuine mistakes as when a player makes a bad clearance or misses a penalty. He doesn't intend to miss penalties or have bad games–it just happens.

The player's attitude towards the referee should, ideally, be as it is towards the captain of his team. If the player makes a really bad decision or makes a terrible error the player must accept it. The best players always do, and this is the same with referees' decisions. If the referee gives something against a player, the better professionals will accept it as one of those things, shrug it off and get on with the game.

The greatest example of this really professional player is Bobby Charlton whom I have admired for years. Nobody wants to win a game more than Bobby and nobody is more determined either but his will to win is reflected in other ways which unfortunately don't attract headlines in the newspapers. Even when a decision is given against Bobby I have never known him to do or say anything that would give the referee cause to have words with

Terry Hennessey (second from the right) playing for Nottingham Forest before his transfer to Derby County.

him–even if he has thought the referee's decision to be a mistake. He just accepts it like a real professional as part of the game.

One thing I do dislike about some referees is a tendency to blow up for comparatively trivial offences but let things which are nasty go by the wayside. But, to be fair, I recognise that referees get involved with the game just as the players do and knowing from experience how different things can appear to be from different angles it has to be recognised that they cannot possibly see everything.

But, having said that, there are a few officials who let players get away with really bad tackles but clamp down hard on what we have come to call "professional fouls", things like *stealing* a few yards at throw-ins or handling the ball that is too high to be headed and could let an opponent in for a clear run to goal.

The really good referees are those who stamp it all out in the first few minutes and making sure that you, the player, know the situation. They make it plain that you either behave or go off for an early bath. All of these top men have one other feature in common too–they treat the players firmly but like grown up, responsible men . . . not like naughty schoolboys. The knack of deciding when to overlook a comparatively minor offence is important too, especially when a whistle would be to the advantage of the offender. But the top men will let you know,

Liverpool goalkeeper Ray Clemence punches clear from Arsenal's Peter Storey.

quietly and firmly, while the game is still going on, that they saw it.

When I first came into the game there used to be quite a lot of talk before matches about the referee. In the dressing room before the game a player would say something about this "fellow being too easy," or, "he doesn't stand any messing about so we'd all better watch ourselves." Today this doesn't happen as much as people might think and I'm sure that the decision to encourage referees to visit the dressing rooms before matches is doing a great deal of good.

For one thing, every referee is different and they all have their own individual method of approach when they get out on the field. This is why the pre-match talk is so helpful because invariably the referee says: "Look, if you have any questions or any doubts, let's get things clarified here before we start." I'm sure, too, that with this increased contact, referees and players have more understanding of each other and the officials are treating the players like men.

The players certainly appreciate this and I think things are getting better every week with fewer players being sent off and less visciousness on the field. If the players and referees can get even closer this can only create understanding of the problems of the two sides and greater respect all round and the game itself will benefit.

This is inevitably more difficult when language barriers are involved but as far as international football is concerned there is a fundamental difference not only between British players and foreign referees but between the two sets of players. This stood out to me in Mexico, where I went as a tourist to see the 1970 World Cup. In the games I saw there were one or two cases where I thought players might have been sent off, but I saw nothing that warranted a penalty. But what stood out was this difference of interpretation between the British and the foreign referees. No matter what anyone says, I'm convinced they have a completely different attitude towards the game and the laws–and this will continue to be a big problem for many years yet.

I'm not suggesting that they are wrong and we are right but it is a fact that foreign players think nothing of pulling your jersey or obstructing you and this infuriates British players–I think because we tend to feel this is a sly way of doing things. Abroad these things are accepted by the players and not dealt with severely by their referees but they annoy a British player more than it would if they took a kick at you.

Obviously we've all got to think afresh for the answer. If we are ever going to find one depends on everyone recognising the fact that a compromise solution has to be found. We've all got to be prepared to go half way to meet the other fellow and reach agreement and better understanding.

Here in Britain we have problems of our own, stemming as I said earlier, from the social revolution that has taken place in the last 20 or 30 years, maybe even longer. It seems to me that we don't accept the police, our parents, teachers or referees. No matter where you look there's less acceptance of discipline nowadays–even in the home. A parent tells a child not to do something and today the kiddies will do exactly what they've been told not to do.

It is in this field that the game has changed in the last 20 years and it is here that the modern referee faces his biggest problem. When a player was fouled in the old days I think they accepted it like men whereas today–myself included–we tend to take it like children and the same is true of hard tackles and free kicks given against us.

Some people blame this on higher wages and bigger win bonuses but to my knowledge money doesn't come into the reckoning with anyone, before, during or after a game. Whether you play for £10 a game or £1,000 it's the last thing you think of on the pitch. Money is nice, of course, when you collect your pay packet the following week and it can buy a lot of things for you and give your family a higher standard of living. But I'm quite sure there's no link between money and any lack of sportsmanship in the game.

The big thing is the game and one's attitude to it and I learned one lesson a long time ago from a referee that I knew personally. He refereed a Cup game I played in years ago and we met before the game and said hello. His language was shocking–almost as bad as mine can be sometimes–and we'd only been on the field two minutes when he gave a free kick against me and I said as I passed him what a "so and so" decision that was. Immediately he had his book out and took my name for bad language!

Half an hour before I'd heard this same man use exactly the same words I'd used but he was a good referee and I respected him even more after that game. Once he'd "booked" me he told me quietly that there were times when I could swear and times when I shouldn't . . . . . . and he was quite right.

(Below) Jackie Charlton of Leeds United takes on two Crystal Palace forwards in the shape of Gerry Queen (9) and Alan Birchenall. (Right) Ian Bowyer of Manchester City eludes a challenge from Jon Sammels (right) of Arsenal.

POLI

OVE KINDVALL says
(of Sweden)

Professional football means a secure future for my family

WHEN I left Sweden to sign as a professional for the Dutch club Feyenoord, I make no bones about it, I was selling myself–signing away four or five years of my life to professional football in exchange for the future of my family. With a wife and two children to think about the only security I know about is £.s.d. and there was little chance of making any real money as a player in amateur Sweden.

Of course, I discussed it all with my wife and we certainly don't regret my joining Feyenoord. In fact, if for any reason we could not return home to Sweden we'd all be quite happy in Holland, but the ties of home keep pulling, and after Feyenoord's incredible European Cup success in 1970 my professional ambitions were fulfilled, my contract obligations were over and we were all set to go.

But officials of the Rotterdam club persuaded me to sign again for just one more year–with increased financial rewards of course–and so it was agreed we stay on.

In May last year I was really on top of the world, although I missed the last month of the season in Holland–Feyenoords' Directors very sportingly released me to join the Swedish squad preparing for the World Cup trip to Mexico. When I left Rotter-

Delighted Feyenoord players parade with the European Cup after their memorable victory over Celtic.

dam I was the top scorer in the Dutch 1st Division, but even more important I had been lucky enough to score the goal that enabled Feyenoord to beat Celtic 2-1 in the European Cup Final and for the first time ever, a Dutch club held the European Cup.

With the excitement of Mexico still to come I was keyed up, but in the World Cup Swedish hopes never quite came off. Looking back I think our problems revolved round two key factors.

Players like myself, Orjan Persson and Ove Grahn had been away from our home-based Swedish team-mates too long. I had adapted my game to suit the style of Feyenoord, as Persson had done with Rangers and we didn't have long enough together to re-adjust ourselves.

Again the problem of the Mexican heat proved a great handicap and no doubt we would have improved in both these basic problems if we'd been able to spend a longer time training together in Mexico. Our results tend to underline this I think, for after two poor games against Israel and Italy we managed to beat Uruguay 1-0 in our third final game and Uruguay, of course, went on to the semi-finals.

In Holland I was accustomed to training every day–every day that is except Sunday (the normal match day) and Mondays–and often in addition to the normal training

sessions which began at 4 p.m. we occasionally did extra training in the mornings.

One of the reasons why we had such a good run in the European Cup was, I think, due to the fact that in Holland's Ere Divisie (Division of Honour) there are only four or five good teams. Most league games are therefore not too difficult and because of this we can save our best performances for the BIG games.

There were other contributory factors, too, of course. One is the extraordinary ability of our centre half, Rinus Israel, who is greatly under-rated in my opinion. I rate him the best stopper in Europe. Our inside left, Wim Van Hanegem, is another fine player, not noticed by the critics because he appeard a little slow but Wim and I have a fine understanding and he's a great player with the ball.

Our Austrian wing half Franz Hasil was another outstanding figure and he was under-rated even by me! In Dutch league games he was quite ordinary, but in the later stages of the European Cup he seemed able to draw on deep, concealed reserves for the big occasions and what a performance he turned in against Celtic!

I don't think that anyone in Holland really thought that we could win the European Cup . . . unless it was our Austrian coach Ernst Happel. Even after we did unusually well in eliminating AC Milan I felt our victory had been due more to the Italians' deficiencies rather than Feyenoord's attributes.

In Italy, almost every team plays the *defend and counter-attack game* and this played into our hands when we met AC Milan in the European Cup. In Rotterdam, the Italians made no attempt to control midfield–they just gave it to us to concentrate on defence. Such circumstances were read-made for Feyenoord and we were in complete control throughout the match. Almost everyone thought this was our best performance but the Italians certainly helped to make it easy.

Celtic were another proposition altogether. I've always liked playing against British teams for although they are hard players, they are, with one or two rare exceptions, also fair and sporting. And

(Left) Bobby Charlton of England and Terry Neill of Northern Ireland lead out their respective teams. (Below) Manchester United centre half Paul Edwards lunges into a tackle against Derek Smethurst of Chelsea with United's Tony Dunne in close attendance.

Celtic, in my opinion, were quite the best team in Britain around 1969-70.

I never really thought that we could beat Celtic but our boss Ernst Happel inspired us all so that we went on to the pitch for the final determined to make Celtic fight all the way. Even at our best it was agreed that we couldn't beat Celtic in a fast open game. That's what Celtic like, of course, and in such circumstances they just go on and on in wave after wave of furious attacks.

So Mr. Happel decided–brilliantly as it turned out–that we would try to keep the ball and slow the game down to a walk. Somehow we made it–helped I am sure by the fact that the Celtic players were a bit too confident and thought it would be easy!

Somehow we struggled along and then suddenly the Feyenoord players appeared to gain in confidence from the fact that our waltz-time tactics were not at all to Celtic's liking. And suddenly in extra time I got a bit of luck–two bits of luck really–and managed to score what proved to be the winning goal. A high ball up the middle looked to me like an easy header for Celtic's McNeil but I chased the ball (just in case).

Then, even after McNeil had missed his header, I was sure the Celtic goalkeeper would come out and smother the ball but luckily for me he hesitated. Suddenly in one stroke the game was won and lost, for there I was between McNeil and his 'keeper, to flick the ball into the net. We'd done it!

Now, after playing in the final stages of the World Cup and helping to win the European Cup, what more ambitions can I have? Now I must think of the future–the future and my family. This is why I must go home to Sweden. If I go home soon, still comparatively young at 28 or 29 I'll be signed by a good club who will help me get a good job outside the game.

And with the money I've made in Holland we'll have our own house and maybe a little over to start some kind of small business. What more can a man ask for? A secure future for his family and a magical memory of scoring the winning goal in extra time of a European Cup Final.

(Left) Leeds United centre forward Mick Jones, a prolific goalscorer both in domestic fare and European competition. (Right) Don Rogers of Swindon Town, generally recognised as the best winger outside the English first division.

If at first you don't succeed . . .

TRY, TRY AND TRY AGAIN!

by IAN HUTCHINSON

(Chelsea striker)

THERE'S an old saying: if at first you don't succeed, try, try, try again. Maybe that's true of most careers in this world, but the trouble with football is that it's essentially a short life and if you don't succeed by the time you're seventeen or so, then there's not much time to keep trying.

You get the occasional man, like Tony Book, the Manchester City skipper, who gets into the big-time late in life–and proceeds to show some of the youngsters what the game is all about.

On the other side of the coin, there are people who eventually make the grade having been rejected out of hand by this club or that–clubs who failed to spot the talent and who later regretted being so short-sighted.

But I doubt if anybody felt more rejected than me.

Ian Hutchinson (10) scores for Chelsea against Aris Solonika.

I couldn't even make the first team at my secondary school in Littleover, Derbyshire. We had a very good side. But I was a big lad, very keen, a defender in those days. It irked me to play second team football. I felt a failure.

Some of my school-mates were in the Derby County junior side and I really envied them. At least they had their sights on a possible career in first-class football. Nobody would give anything at all for a lad languishing in his school's reserve side.

So I left school and went to work in a factory. They had a works team, operating in a local amateur league, so I joined and carried on playing as a wing-half or a full-back. I was tall, so the defence looked the best bet for me.

Anyway, my luck changed just for a while. The club recommended me to Nottingham Forest and for a season and a half I played for their junior and 'A' sides. Nobody actually told me that I had no hope of making the grade. They just stopped playing me in matches. I had to take the hint. It was back to International Combustion First XI for me.

A very successful works side. So successful that I couldn't get in their defence–and it was then that I decided to try my luck once more as an attacker. It worked. I started getting the goals.

I became a part-time professional with Burton Albion in 1967. Then on to Cambridge United. Then, just for a change, my luck turned. All my try, try, try again business paid off. Chelsea's coach

West Ham's Tommy Taylor (left) cuts out a ball from Chelsea's Peter Houseman (11).

then was Frank Blunstone, the former England winger, and he turned up to watch our goal-keeper, Chris Barker.

He spared a few glances for me. I had a pretty fair game that day. Later, the assistant manager Ron Suart came along, then finally manager Dave Sexton. They put in a bid for me. I joined Chelsea, for £2,500 or thereabouts. Another similar sum was to be paid if I had more than twelve first team games.

It was hardly the most sensational of transfers. If I felt a shade more confident about making soccer my career, I certainly wasn't wildly optimistic. I knew all about that fantastic pool of talent they have at Stamford Bridge.

But when rejects make the grade, they attract the bargain-buy does it again sort of headlines. At last, I felt I was in with a chance–but I still qualified as a maintenance engineer, just in case.

Now I've knocked in quite a few goals, and knocked at the door of international recognition. The strange thing is that now I'm in a handy position in the professional game, so many people apparently feel sorry for me.

That stems from the "stick" I take from defenders. And a lot of people know that I'm virtually a regular in the Chelsea "casualty" department on Sunday mornings during the season. I regard it as my job to get in there in positions where I might easily get hurt.

Of course the First Division is tough. But it's my view that it was a darned sight tougher in the Southern League where there are a lot of ageing old professionals who really do know a trick or two to deal with aggressive young upstarts!

I believe that people who take no risks at all are pretty dull. In First Division football these days, the chances of scoring are more scarce than ever before, so you must go in, like a bull at a gate if you have the strength, in chasing every chance. So the goals have come. Virtually everybody in the Chelsea side can score goals, and even goalkeeper Peter Bonetti fancies himself as a penalty-taker–but I've had more than my fair share of memorable goals. One specially good one was in an away game with Everton, when John Hollins put a low ball through the middle and I moved up to beat both Brian Labone and Tommy Wright before letting one go.

But nothing can match our Cup Final with Leeds, which came at the end of my first full season with the club. There was first the Wembley drawn game, drawn at 2–2. That game above all showed the fantastic fight-back spirit Chelsea have developed under Dave Sexton. Twice we came back. Both Peter Houseman and I scored on our first-ever appearances at Wembley. I slept very well indeed that night. . . .

And then the replay at Old Trafford–which anyway was a history-making thing in itself. It was Chelsea's firs

Alan Hudson, an outstanding prospect for Chelsea and England.

vin in the FA Cup, and the club had been trying since 1905. Again Leeds went ahead and we wondered if we weren't pushing our luck thinking that we could hit back yet again. But Peter Osgood dived in for the equaliser.

Then just one minute before half-time in extra time, I got in a long throw. Up went the heads and in went defender David Webb to slam the ball in from the approximate area of his left cheek-bone.

This long throw of mine has given me plenty more headlines. I can reach 115 ft., roughly speaking. I've been criticised on the grounds that it's some kind of foul throw, but I'm content to leave referees and linesmen to decide on that. Yet it was purely an accident that we found out I could throw a ball.

We were all lined up during training and told to practice throws. I reached further than the others–actually John Hollins was previously the boy for the long throw. So I worked on it. Used properly it can be as good as a corner–despite the moans that it creates a sort of gimmicky dead-ball situation. Of course, if I'm taking the throw in, I cannot be in the middle to meet it . . . though I'm working on that very problem!

But if finding that long throw was an accident, then I'm for once glad that I'm accident prone.

The role of the out-and-out striker may be getting harder to play as the game goes on, but I'm working on all the different attributes. You must have speed, must be able to control a ball, must time a jump properly, and must be able to read the game accurately. Get all that together and you end up with a Geoff Hurst or a Ron Davies–two players I admire very much indeed.

All the same, anybody playing in a competitive sport has to be realistic. I could wind up with a bad injury–so often it is the striker who gets the worst end of the deal. People reckoned I was being pessimistic when I insisted on going through with my five-year apprenticeship as a maintenance engineer, and I hope they are right.

But when you've had as many rejections in a sporting career as I have, you realise that it's better to be safe than sorry.

Keith Weller, a Chelsea signing from Millwall, has emerged as a regular goalscorer in the English first division.

Talent alone is not enough for the top level today

by BRYAN ROBSON

(West Ham United)

BORN and bred in the North East, I was steeped in the tradition of top quality players being readily available at any pit-head and even today when I would have thought that everyone could see that skill alone was no longer enough, there are still many people who refuse to accept that the game has changed or that the "old style" was best. At the same time, however, I have found a growing number of people developing a greater interest than ever before and while the game is attracting more and more attention, too many youngsters seem to think that talent alone is enough to make a player into a star.

I remember reading one of Gary Player's books about golf and the one thing that I recall above all else was his statement that . . . "my greatest ability is my dedication to practice." Talented boys today seem to think they have gold in their feet–that playing football is easy money. But if the higher financial rewards being offered today are attainable by all–success is the standard set and brings the biggest financial rewards–I agree wholeheartedly with Gary Player.

In my opinion, no player can ever practise too much. The higher you go, the more successful you and your club are, the higher the rewards; but as you go further in the game and become more successful the standards get higher and winning becomes far more difficult than spectators can possibly imagine. As I see it, only those players–outstanding though they may be as individuals with the ball–that dedicate themselves in training and in their private lives off the field will ever reach the top.

Don't run away with the idea that because of this attitude as outlined above, or because I helped Newcastle United win the Fairs Cup, that I think I've reached the top. I don't think I've hit my peak yet but after ten years as a full time professional and still only 27 I feel I'm learning and improving all the time. In my first season as a pro with Newcastle in 1964/65 we were champions of the Second Division and promoted and with the club back in its rightful place in the top class most of my professional career has been spent in the First Division.

Even in my time the game has changed enormously and as a consequence I've had to adapt my *style* of play, too. It's this that brings home to players just how much thought is going into the game today, for I started out as a striker and found myself forced back, deeper into midfield.

This wasn't any change of tactics or an order or suggestion from our manager, Mr. Joe Harvey, but simply a question of being forced to change my game. I'm sure that as far as the club was concerned I was still regarded as a striker and I feel my talents are best suited to an attacking, scoring role. But I found over a period of time in the First Division that as marking got tighter and the tackling quicker, I simply had to drop deeper into midfield.

If I waited upfield for the ball I was tackled from behind, often chopped down and very frequently dispossessed or even prevented from receiving the pass aimed for me. So I slipped a little deeper and found that defenders detailed to tight-mark me were reluctant to come too far and there was a point in mid-field where I could position myself in relatively free space.

Such a place doesn't really exist in the speed of the game today, but like everything else it's relative. Where I felt that lying upfield I could be marked out of a game, I now found it easier to pick up the ball and play as a striker by taking up deeper positions. To put it into a few simple words–I was forced to go deeper to get the ball.

In the last few months with Newcastle, I found myself in midfield quite regularly and I can imagine that for spectators it is probably

Jeff Astle of West Bromwich Albion and England.

very difficult to say whether I was playing as a striker, or as a worker in midfield, in any particular game. I know myself through these experiences that the game has changed and that my approach (and my game) have changed too, but one thing that hasn't changed is my dedication.

I know, too, through conversation with my colleagues–other players and personal friends–that interest generally is developing more deeply in the game as a whole. Playing or watching–but more particularly playing–you are constantly made aware of new ideas in the most forceful way. This is the most painful way to learn, when the opposition produce some new twist or move at a corner or a free kick, but we at Newcastle tried to introduce our share of innovations. This is how the game progresses with one team thinking up something new and another club coming along either to counter it completely or to give it an even more modern touch. Generally I would say that people in Britain are paying more attention to coaching and taking a deeper interest in the game itself. Certainly football has never before been taken so seriously or produced such consistently good results for British teams.

Compared with Britain my experience of Continental teams is that they don't like to go forward. We can all see that in many cases Continental players have greater individual ability than their British counterparts but it appears to me that the bulk of foreign teams are afraid of losing, scared to concede a goal and as a consequence their players get orders to "stay goal-side of the ball". Even if this fear that I have seen and sensed playing against foreign teams is not the result of a direct order from their boss, the players generally look to me to be scared. Worried about going forward in case they lose the ball and get the blame if a goal is scored against them, many very good foreign players use their skills and talent in a negative way–like the Italians.

This was particularly true of the Portuguese clubs Newcastle met. Sporting Lisbon, Porto FC and Vitoria Setubal all had some very good players but generally they wasted their skill by trying to play keep-the-ball, giving each other *square passes* in midfield . . . and getting square balls back. All they

Derby County centre forward John O'Hare has made rapid strides during the past two seasons and has won a number of Scottish caps.

Blackpool goalkeeper Alan Taylor saves from Jimmy Greaves of West Ham with former England skipper Jim Armfield lending a willing boot to the Blackpool cause.

managed most of the time was to retain possession.

Strangely enough, bearing in mind the Italians' reputation for negative football, the only team that really tried to contain us and give us trouble in our Fairs Cup matches was FC Internazionale. Sandro Mazzola was the key man, a centre or inside forward, whose ability showed up for everyone who watched the 1970 World Cup even on TV. Mazzola was the only player we met who had the confidence and the ability to run at our defence with the ball on his own. He varied his approach, too, sometimes using his footwork to beat men but often laying off the ball and going away looking for a return pass–and he really was quick on the break.

The Brazilians are an obvious exception to what I've said about foreign players and I was personally very disappointed last season when, after Newcastle had been involved in discussions about the possibilities of taking part in a friendly tournament against Glasgow Celtic and Santos FC, it all fell through.

From what I've heard the Brazilian game at home has genuine wingers and I know that many people in this country thought that Brazil used old-style wingers in the World Cup in Mexico. I saw quite clearly that left winger Rivelino has a tremendous left foot shot–he used it often and scored a few goals too–while "right winger" Jairzinho was frequently inside the opponents' penalty area, sometimes even on the left flank in striking positions.

(Above) Cyril Knowles and Pat Jennings of Tottenham Hotspur keep out the tenacious figure of Leeds United captain Billy Bremner. (Right) Burnley's Colin Waldron robs Alan Gilzean (right) of Spurs at White Hart Lane.

But Rivelino spent a great deal of time and effort *working* in midfield and though I recognise that Jairzinho was a striker, to me neither of them was a real old-fashioned winger in the fullest sense.

On television you can only see what the cameraman shows you and that was why I was so disappointed when the chance to get a close-up look at the Brazilians fell through. I wanted to see it all for myself, to get the "feel" of their game out on the park and get the chance to see how some of these great Brazilian stars like Pele coped with English-style close marking and quick tackling.

In particular, I would like to see how Pele would counter, or avoid, tackling from behind and going "over the ball." These two factors I am sure, play a big part in preventing good young British players from really developing their skills but as things stand now they cannot be stamped out. Under the Laws of the game (as they are interpreted in Britain at least) they are OK and referees generally don't pay enough attention in my opinion to the kind of defenders who try to go *through* an opponent's legs to get the ball.

That, of course, is out of my province. It's up to the International Board to amend the Laws or the referees to change their interpretation, but the fact still remains that I was really looking forward to seeing how Pele got on against British teams over here. I'm sure I'd have learned something from him–and that's what the game is about . . . learning by observation, working in training and dedication.

Celtic - the best I've seen in Europe...

says Anatoli Bychewecz (U.S.S.R.)

FOOTBALL is getting better all the time, even if it does appear at times after tough defensive battles that the pleasures of playing and watching are on the wane. The problems, and the hopes for a brighter future, revolve around the fact that everyone knows each other too well–their strengths and their weaknesses.

This is inevitable in these days of international competition and the top trainers spying on each other before the big games. But these meetings, so common nowadays, are leading the game forward . . . and upward.

In my time with Dynamo Kiev's first team and the national team of the USSR I have no doubt that our game is getting better. Our results suggest this but the fact that we've never yet won some of the most sought after competitions is explained (to our regret) by the fact that other teams in other parts of Europe are making progress too.

This I'm sure, is a natural process–the evolution of football. Travel, experience and competition lead to greater understanding. New ideas are copied and following these new ideas is a new surge of development. Today the national team players of Spain, England, the USSR and Austria know just about as much about each other as they do of the club sides who play in their own national leagues.

Personally I dislike defensive football. Being a forward, and one who likes to score goals, this is quite natural, but we must see the defender's viewpoint too. If I like to get goals, my opponents want to stop me. This is what the game and its evolution

Anatoli Bychewecz, a fan of Scottish club Celtic.

Mexico's Pulido leaps high to head for goal, challenged by Russian captain Shesternev (left) and Logofet.

are all about. The answer, in my opinion, is quite simple–the individuals must get better, not only more skilled and quicker, but more adept at reproducing their skills in match play; quicker to spot an opening being made by a colleague, quicker to take advantage of an opponent's defensive error.

Until now it seems at times that my whole life has been bound up in sport, and football in particular, but I wouldn't want to change it. As a boy I was always playing football whenever I had the chance and at 12 I joined the Dynamo Kiev club's boys school. In addition to all the usual subjects, football received a high place in the school curriculum. Usually there are between 80 and 100 youngsters at the "Kiev soccer school" and about 80% of the time allotted to football is spent on improving their skills, while the other 20% is devoted to allied sports aimed at building up speed and condition.

When I was 16 years old I left school to join the Dynamo Kiev club where the chief trainer was Victor Maslov. He led the club to three consecutive successes in the championship of the USSR in 1966, 1967 and 1968. I had made my debut for Dynamo in 1964 when I was 18 and by 1966 I was a regular first team choice and was therefore able to enjoy my share of this treble success. In the 1966 season I was hoping to be the top scorer in the USSR but finally finished with 19 goals–one less than Dynamo

West German goalkeeper Sepp Maier is now established as one of Europe's leading custodians.

Tbilissi's Datunaschwili. So far that was my most successful season in goalscoring terms and since then I've never even finished second highest scorer again.

After leaving school I studied in Kiev at the Institute of Physical Culture, gaining my diploma at the end of 1970 and with this behind me I'll stay in sport when my playing career is over–teaching all sports from basketball to football.

The best club teams I've played against in international competitions are, without doubt, Celtic and the Gornik Zabrze club of Poland. Both these teams beat us in the European Cup, but I must say I thought Celtic were a little bit fortunate when we played them last in Glasgow. Even so they are a fine team and I was really surprised when they were beaten in the 1970 European Cup Final by Feyenoord.

We were a bit unlucky, too, when we lost to Gornik Zabrze–who beat us in Kiev 2–1! They caught us at the end of an exhausting season in which we had to struggle for the championship again, playing 38 league games and four Russian

Kakhi Asatiani, one of the most exciting prospects to emerge in the Soviet Union in recent years.

Cup games between March and November. Then at the end of that run came Gornik.

In the USSR our national league clubs are spread over enormous distances. And people who say the problems of a European League are insoluble because of the travelling this would involve should take a look at the travel schedules of Russian clubs. We play the equivalent of a European League every season.

At home in the USSR we travel to all away league games by plane and even in the days of the big super-fast modern jets it still takes us five hours to fly the enormous distances to Taschkent and Alma Ata. Personally I'm not too keen on travelling but in some weeks we play three games–maybe in Alma Ata on Sunday, Kiev on Wednesday and then Leningrad the following Sunday. In between, it is just possible to arrange a training session but because this always has to be the day before a game or the day after, it can never be more than a light run out.

Only in winter is really heavy training possible unless we go abroad on tour with the club or the national team. At home in Kiev the season starts in late March or early April, usually in rain and not snow. But at the end of the season in November the temperature drops well below freezing and we finish our league fixtures on snow or ice.

Then, though we do get away now and again in the season to see our families and friends we usually have the luxury of a month off in December. Then the pre-season fitness training begins again, usually ski-ing or skating. One thing though. Well wrapped up and working hard–it's never cold.

But if life can be difficult for football players in the USSR, with so little time to spare for one's families, the really difficult job is done by the people who arrange the fixture lists. Fitting in 38 league games between April and November–as well as leaving blanks for the national team matches–and allowing time for travelling the enormous distances involved is a real man-sized job.

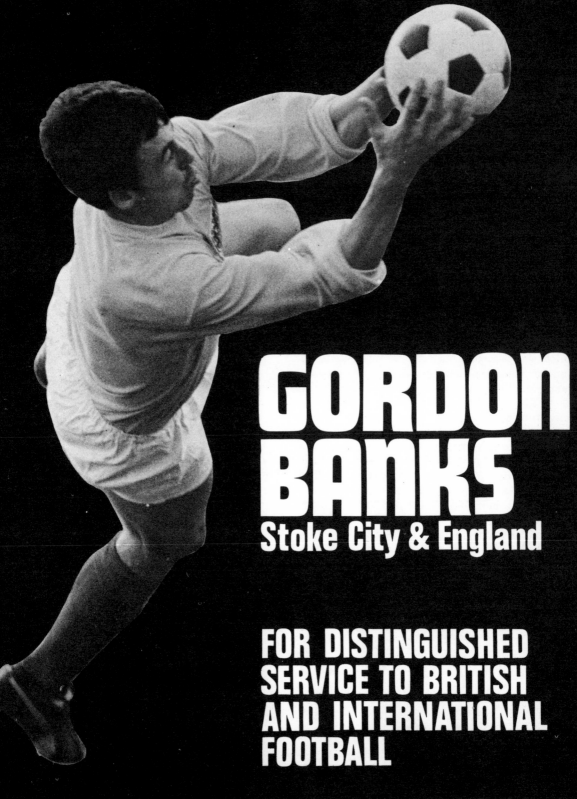

FOOTBALL SWORD OF HONOUR 1971

GORDON BANKS

Stoke City & England

FOR DISTINGUISHED SERVICE TO BRITISH AND INTERNATIONAL FOOTBALL

ANY one attempting to draw up a list of the all-time great goalkeepers of the post war period would be sure to include Frank Swift, of Manchester City and England, Lev Yashin, who starred for years with Dynamo Moscow and the USSR, and Ladislao Mazurkiewiecz whose performances for Penarol and Uruguay had placed him on the World number one pedestal when Gordon Banks staked his claim in 1966.

All three were essentially different types of goalkeeper: Swift–a superlative combination of brilliance and showmanship; Yashin whose every movement bore the stamp of unadulterated class and Mazurkiewiecz's talents being a blend of superb anticipation, handling and agility. To see any of these three just once–near their peak–was to be persuaded immediately of their claim to fame, but with Gordon Banks the way to the top was long and hard.

Looking back it seems inconceivable that Banks, first capped for England in 1963, was still being challenged for his England place by Tony Waiters of Blackpool in 1964 and it was only one year before the 1966 World Cup that he made the position his own. Even then his greatest asset seemed to be consistency and it was only during the 1966 World Cup when he played such a vital role in the England success that he suddenly *arrived*.

"In goals", as Gordon himself would put it, doing the simple things well and not giving away soft goals by mishandling or being caught out of position are the mark of a good goalkeeper. This and an ability to talk well–calling to his colleagues when he wants a ball left for him, and saying it loud and clear in good time–leads to reliability. This, in turn, breeds confidence in the defence and bounces back to the man between the sticks in the form of respect for him and his ability to read the game. With a colleague under pressure, a word from Banks and the ball is en route to his hands and the command 'anywhere' shouted at just the right moment when a defender was in two minds has got many a colleague out of difficulty and prevented innumerable goal-chances from ever arising.

It's all too easy when recalling the 1966 World Cup to remember Geoff Hurst's hat trick in the final and the memorable goals hit by Bobby Charlton in

Gordon Banks . . . recipient of the International Football Book's Sword of Honour for 1971.

Throughout the world Gordon Banks (left) has earned a reputation for his skill and sportsmanship.

the earlier matches but in the excitement of the 1966 series the dependability of Gordon Banks was consistently under-rated. Only when the competition was over and the World Cup safely locked away at Lancaster Gate did the game as a whole suddenly become aware that 'Banksee' had done well.

But in the semi-final alone, Banks' performance against an out of touch Portuguese side that had played brilliantly in earlier matches made the difference between victory and defeat. In goal for Portugal, Jose Pereira gave away a soft goal when he came out well, almost to the edge of his own penalty area to go down for a long through pass. Pereira intercepted all right, got his body behind the ball but inexplicably failed to hold it and while he lay on the ground at the edge of the box the ball rolled loose to present Bobby Charlton with a gift goal.

Near the end of that same match after Portugal had pulled back to 1–2 and were pressing for an equaliser, their superb captain and midfield general Mario Coluna moved upfield himself. Receiving the ball from a corner on the right wing, Coluna shaped up to cross the ball, then pushing it forward to the edge of the area suddenly let fly with one of his 'flat-footed', curling, dipping, chip-cum-drives. Hit as it was over a crowded penalty area, Banks could never have got the *early* sight of the ball that enables a good 'keeper to be on his way and turn a good high shot over the bar. With the ball right up on top of him before he saw it Banks had to produce a reflex action to palm the ball over. In all the excitement few people stopped to think that, on the day, if the two sides had changed goalkeepers then it would almost certainly have been Portugal who would have gone on to meet West Germany in the final.

Banks had now arrived, establishing him almost overnight when a complex blend of ability, hard training and experience suddenly compounded itself to push him up amongst the all-time greats. In the four years that followed his reputation grew almost match by match and in 1970 when the Mexico World Cup began Gordon Banks was acknowledged, almost throughout the World, as the top custodian of the time.

Certainly there was no one to match him amongst the other 15 countries in the World Cup, and even reputable players like Bulgaria's Simeonov and Viktor of Czechoslovakia returned home slightly less well thought of. With Yashin still active but clearly past his best perhaps Italy's Zoff is Banks' closest challenger, though the Italian team manager preferred Albertosi.

But of even greater importance is the fact that all the teams who did really well (with the exception of Uruguay) . . . Brazil, West Germany and Italy were

Emlyn Hughes of Liverpool has filled both full back positions in the England team.

all desperately lacking a really top grade goalkeeper.

Thirty-one years old in Mexico, there is evidence that Banks has still to strike his peak and the save he made against a header from Pelé in the England-Brazil match had to be seen to be believed. Pelé's header, powered *down* from around the six or seven yard mark, was almost perfection itself, bouncing as it did at the foot of Banks' right post. Having been lured to the near-post by the Brazilian buildup, Banks had to re-position himself when the expected shot did not materialise and the save–knocking the ball down so hard that it bounced not only round the post but also high above the crossbar–can only be described as miraculous.

Through the wonders of the film camera and the aid of a friend well versed in the number of 'frames' taken per minute by a movie camera, counting the frames from Pelé's header to Banks' save reveals the unbelievable information that it took the England 'keeper only 3/5ths of a second to see, move and save!

'Keepers, of course, have never yet been known to win games single handed but it is a fact that a brilliant performance by a goalkeeper can so hearten his colleagues and create such dismay amongst the opposition that they can influence the results of matches to a fantastic degree. And without wishing to knock Banks' England deputy, Peter Bonetti, who stood in for him when the Stoke City star was attacked by the **Mexican tummy** and couldn't play in the quarter final in which West Germany beat England 3–2 after being two goals down, I will for ever be convinced that it couldn't have happened if Banks had been there.

With Mexico behind him and many another world famous professional soccer player having been made a *personality* by press and television, becoming half pro-half businessman, Banks remains satisfied in industrial Staffordshire. Apparently unconscious of the fame he has gained and the money this could bring him he dedicates himself to his training with the enthusiasm of a youngster still to make a mark–too busy concentrating on his next game for Stoke City to be interested in commerce and the bright lights. With that kind of attitude Gordon Banks will surely remain the World's number one 'keeper for some years to come.

ERIC G. BATTY

Bob Stokoe, appointed manager of Blackpool at the beginning of 1971, had previously been in charge of Bury, Charlton Athletic, Rochdale and Carlisle.

I have been a wanderer

by GRAHAM MOORE

(Wales and Charlton)

DURING my career, which really started with a League appearance for Cardiff City against Fulham some fourteen years ago, I've been a wanderer. A Welsh wanderer. Some players stick with one club and all is well for them, but others get this reputation for being nomadic by instinct.

I went from Cardiff to Chelsea to Manchester United to Northampton Town (when they were in Division One) and to Charlton Athletic.

If travel broadens the mind, then I'm one of the most broad-minded fellows in the business.

The travelling hasn't really done me much harm as far as winning Welsh caps are concerned, because I was "capped" while with each of my clubs. But if being a Welsh wanderer hasn't really done me any harm, the fact is that the odds are so much stacked against Wales really emerging as an international force.

Take the international championship at the end of the 1969/70 season. We may have only scored two goals, though we conceded only one–but we still notched four points, enough to give us a tie with the "more favoured" Scots and English. But for us to really emerge as an international power, we've got to make up for our shortage of class players with a whole lot more co-operation in getting those players released for duty in the red shirts of Wales.

In that particular end-of-season campaign in the summer of 1970, we held England to a 1–1 draw at Cardiff. That, surely, was enough to prove that given a fair break we have the talent. Dick Krzywicki got our goal and Martin Peters bobbed up to score for England.

Playing with an eleven that included Mike England, Ron Davies, Tony Millington, Terry Hennessey, the fast-rising Rod Thomas and so on, showed that Welsh fervour really isn't confined to the Rugby fields. That's one problem, of course–so many youngsters taking up rugger at school and then sticking with it.

My own belief is that if Wales could stay free from injuries AND get time for players to become acclimatised to the whole atmosphere of big-time international football, we'd do very well indeed. It depends on co-operation, of course. Maybe one can't blame an English manager of an English League club for underestimating the importance of Welsh soccer.

Maybe some proof comes from the fact that after holding England we were able to field the same team for the next game–and went to Hampden Park, Glasgow, and held Scotland to a goal-less draw. The same team again did duty at Swansea and we beat Northern Ireland by a Ronnie Rees' goal to nil.

A mixture of youth and experience, plus that fighting spirit and not even the magic of Georgie Best could do us down.

But at Christmas-time in 1967, I reckoned I could be out of the game for good. A diabolical stab of pain in my back . . . and the next thing I remember is specialists tut-tutting around me and looking very grim-faced indeed.

I had an operation and they removed a disc from my backbone and I had to endure months of waiting and hoping before it was found that my wandering career could go on.

At first I felt dispirited. When you get an injury like that, you wonder just how hard you can go before you get a recurrence. In the end, though, I threw myself whole-heartedly into training–I reckon I worked harder than at any stage during my career.

Looking back, I suppose I was that bit lazier in my pre-Charlton days. Mind you, we worked terribly hard at Chelsea under Tommy Docherty–I was brought in to add punch to his front-line, but things didn't work out exactly as planned! Generally, though I found that being in the top class, with top clubs, I got that feeling that things couldn't go wrong, so that it wasn't so necessary to put every-

Graham Moore, a Welsh wanderer who has given service to a number of League clubs.

Graham Moore, in action for Charlton Athletic, against Lionel Martin of Aston Villa.

thing into the training sessions.

At Charlton Athletic, things have been pretty dreadful in recent seasons. I went into that aforementioned international campaign with a fair amount of nervous strain hanging over me–the club, and I was skipper, had escaped relegation from the Second Division by the skin of our teeth.

Crowds, at international or club level, are entitled to demand success and some of the followers of Charlton felt they'd suffered more than enough. Nothings worse than turning out in front of a small crowd, specially when that crowd finds it hard to raise any enthusiasm.

At least, though, I had showed through well enough in a defensive mid-field role to get those extra Welsh caps–not the last, I hope, because nothing gives more satisfaction than playing for one's country. I've read of some players who feel that their clubs pay the wages so they should always have first call. Well, I don't see any reason why a player shouldn't produce the same loyalty and dedication to his country as well.

Even so, there's no doubt that it's harder to stay in the international picture when you are playing for a struggling club. I don't mind that. I love the challenge of working for Charlton. And, as I said before, Wales are not so well off for players that they can actually overlook any players of even remote international class.

I've played against Chile and Hungary and Italy, plus a commemorative game against the United Kingdom. That's given me a good look at football round the world, as well as my travels round the English League clubs. At all levels, there's no doubt the game has tightened up tactically and in a lot of ways it has become much harder.

Seeing it at first hand has simply turned me further away from the play-actors–the characters who pretend all sorts of things from severe injury to injured innocence. Football has to be a game of physical contact, otherwise it loses its style, and its drama.

When I was a striker, going hell-for-leather for goal chances, I got kicked around a lot. I got into tight situations and it was man-against-man after the ball. When I moved back into mid-field, either in attack or defence, I still got kicked. All right, sometimes I kicked back. It's all part of the game, be it an international or a middle-of-the-table League game.

But there is no point in squealing. You have your own remedies within the laws of the game, and I'm quite sure the fans don't want to see those expressive displays of hurt and injury that sometimes even get referees blowing up the wrong way.

Travelling round the country, as it were, I've been involved with some excellent managers. Sir Matt Busby, at Manchester United, ran club affairs one way. Tommy Docherty, at Chelsea, had his way in a different manner. At Northampton with their remarkable record of up-and-down behaviour, the Welsh national team manager Dave Bowen was in control–and he and I think very much the same way about football.

Of course I've had my own ups and downs as a player. But, looking back from a ripe old age (I'm only joking, because I have years ahead of me yet), I'm pleased to be involved with young talent coming through. Lads develop so early these days–mastering the different skills while still in the apprentice class. If they're good enough, they're old enough . . . the adage is more true than ever.

I was seventeen when I first got into League football. A year later, they were hailing me as the new wonder boy of Welsh soccer. Winning that first international cap remains a fantastic thrill.

Each new game for Wales brings more excitement. Look down the home international championship results and you can see the obvious problems facing Wales. You can probably think of quite a few really outstanding Welshmen, world-class stars, but finding a full eleven to match their abilities is not so easy.

We shared the championship in 1959/60. And in 1955/56, and again four years before that. But you have to go back to the 1930's, our golden years in a way, to find Wales outright winners. We had three wins in that decade–back in the days before I was even born.

In the main, though, it's regarded as a two-horse race between Scotland and England. I've a feeling all that is going to change now. We've some great youngsters coming through. Plus a bit of strength at the back in terms of experience.

A certain Northern Ireland international of world fame has said that he regrets not being English born only at World Cup time. He feels his country has too much stacked against it to qualify for the Finals.

Well, I don't think it would take a miracle for Wales to go through to Munich in 1974. Just a bit of luck to go with the skills we can produce.

And a bit of luck after all this time isn't too much to ask for, is it?

Wolves goalkeeper Phil Parkes looks relieved as he watches the ball skim the post during a match between Chelsea and Wolves. Dave Webb (right) is the Chelsea player.

Ron McKinnon (Glasgow Rangers and Scotland) is beaten to the ball by Geoff Hurst (West Ham United and England).

BOOT IS ON THE OTHER FOOT . . .

by PETER JONES

NOT so long ago, it was the done thing in show-business circles to fling a Press reception to tell the Great British Public just what was going on. Journalists stood around supping free drinks and eating small bits of dead fish on toast.

Fair enough. It gave the star, starlet or plain nonentity a chance to air his or her ego. They talked non-stop about their aims and ambitions. Hear one nonentity spouting nonsense and you've heard them all.

But times change. The Press receptions still go on, but now the stars talk...soccer! Because I write both show business and soccer, I get the questions from both sides. Top soccer players seem fascinated by the bright lights of pop, films and stage.

Show-business personalities are interested in what I can tell them about the soccer giants. A pop-singing friend of mine is now a hero in the eyes of his young son simply because he accidentally took a telephone call to me from–George Best!

Jimmy Tarbuck predictably rabbits on about his beloved Liverpool. He has a twenty-minute script always available about the latest sayings of manager Bill Shankly. The players are his personal friends.

His latest story: "It was a Fourth Division match, played on a Tuesday evening. Suddenly the floodlights failed and the game was abandoned. Said

Luton Town manager Alec Stock . . . and behind him comedian Eric Morecambe, a director of Luton.

COM1C
DB
6

this supporter: 'Obviously–bad play stopped light!'"

There was an on location reception for a new Richard Attenborough film–he was directing and starring. Through it all, he looked worried, instead of wearing the usual PRO-smiling expression. We asked him if he was behind schedule on shooting or something else financially disastrous. "Oh, no", he said. "I've just heard that Peter Osgood is out of Saturday's game."

Richard Attenborough is on the board of directors of Chelsea.

Pop group the Hollies were due to tour Australia in the height of summer, down under. A dream trip. First-class travel and hotels, and paid for their trouble. But it grieved rhythm guitarist Terry Sylvester. "Don't you know we leave the day before the Third Round of the Cup?", he demanded. "And I've got a ticket to see Liverpool versus Aldershot."

For him, it was a personal crisis. His Liverpool "lovelies" might be against Fourth Division opposition, but he felt a traitor because he couldn't be there to urge them on.

Ken Dodd will talk comedy until the cows, or at least the milk, comes home. He keeps note-books on different jokes and how they go down with audiences. But he's got other books with every available detail about Liverpool–and he's even operated as a scout with them.

Ed Stewart, one of the most popular disc-jockeys, known as "Stewpot" to a million kids, had a Press reception to announce his new television series. He got the business over quickly. What he wanted most was to chat me up and see if I could get him a couple of tickets for Arsenal–Everton, knowing that I was due to meet Alan Ball the evening before.

And there's John Alderton, star of television's "Please Sir", in which he plays schoolmaster Bernard Hedges. Yet as a kid he played truant to watch his Hull City favourites. He appeared at a Press reception for Tom Courtenay, that world-noted film star. Immediately the subject of conversation was Hull City–and Tom revealed that he'd even named his dog Waggy, after Hull City star Ken Wagstaff.

John even went to Mexico to see the World Cup

(Left) famous show-business personality, Jimmy Tarbuck, is a fanatical Liverpool supporter. (Right) another Liverpudlian comic, Ken Dodd.

finals of 1970, even though it meant turning down some well-paid work.

There's Eric Morecambe, partner of Ernie Wise, and rated one of the funniest men in the world. Eric, "the one with glasses", had a heart attack and had to take things easy. He became a director of Luton Town, which is hardly the best way to relax. But he says, deadly serious: "I find the atmosphere of soccer a complete therapy for my life in show business."

And not so serious, he tells the one about the goalkeeper who kept missing high balls pumped into his area. Shouted one supporter: "He is like Dracula –he hates crosses!"

What about Roy Castle, as contender for the Top Supporter award? He felt sick at having to wear contact lenses because of failing eyesight. Sick, that is, until he found out that his hero, Nobby Stiles of Manchester United, also wore them when playing! But Roy is a Huddersfield Town fan. So is former Prime Minister Harold Wilson–when Harold held one of his parties at Number Ten, he spent quite a lot of time talking soccer to Bobby Charlton, George Best, Kenny Lynch and others. Visiting diplomats were there, but diplomacy could wait while Leeds United's chase for the League title was properly analysed.

And so it goes on. Show-business people get together ostensibly to talk about their own careers, but get quickly into the real business of discussing the world of football. Show folk are just about the most fanatical of all over the game.

What they ask me mostly is: "What sort of a bloke IS George Best?" And I tell them that despite the pressures piled on him, both on the field and off, he's a likeable, rather shy, friendly sort of soul, but that geniuses are also human beings.

Either that or they take the mickey if Chelsea happen to come up with a bad result.

But then we journalists are a totally unprejudiced lot. I mean, it's purely by accident that the name-plate outside my house reads: CHELBRIDGE!

Ken Dodd, a director of Runcorn FC, with his assistants, the Diddymen, give a demonstration of tactics.

I.F.B.

EDITORIAL

TO the multitudes who have been caught by the football bug, whether we have the comfort of a season ticket at our favourite club or a precarious foothold on the terraces, there is a privileged class–the journalist. Without exception they are the object of envy, the "lucky" ones who jet around the world to see all the international matches and the four-yearly "holiday" at World Cup time.

To our friends who watch the series nowadays at home on television via satellite it is impossible to convey any idea of the problems and discomforts which the *lucky* journalist has to suffer. But with the Mexico World Cup fresh enough in the mind and knowing full well that via TV the fans at home were kept right up to date with regard to injuries, team selection and FIFA decisions, this seems an appropriate time to try and bridge the gap of understanding between the fans–readers of the International Football Book–and the working journalist. It might also come to the attention of FIFA officials, who let it be said have made enormous strides forward in recent years in their bid to ease the problems of the Press.

There are, let it be said quite clearly, two classes of football journalist just as there are at least two basic groups of fans. The first class of (journalist and fan) sets out with the intention of following their team to the final and for them with all the expertise of the modern travel agent, reinforced by the experience and ever developing ideas of FIFA, the road is comparatively smooth. For these fans a World Cup is indeed a holiday and for this category of journalist there are only two additional hazards to counter in addition to the usual problems which go hand in hand with his job even at home. These of course are language difficulties and the communication problem which can be quite a headache with his newspaper 5,000 miles away or more and everyone wanting to use the telephone at more or less the same time.

For the second category of football writer and the more adventurous neutral fan–neutral perhaps because his team has been unfortunate and failed to qualify–the World Cup can be, as the Americans say . . . "something else".

West Ham United full back or midfield player Billy Bonds.

With a temporary home-cum-office set up in Mexico City (a hotel room) supplemented superbly by the facilities organised for the Press by FIFA, we attempt to "see as much as possible." Interviews with managers and players; watching training sessions, and commuting from centre to centre to watch what we hope will be the most interesting game on each of the days set aside for matches. Extra time can be a nightmare, throwing out plane or train schedules and in Mexico "Montezuma's Revenge" the tummy troubles which attacked practically every foreign visitor was an additional hazard, somehow managing to strike each individual at the most inconvenient time.

In Mexico, where the organisers wisely limited the match venues to an area of something less than 20% of the country as a whole, transport was still the biggest headache inevitably bringing out the question: "Why should FIFA stage a World Cup series in countries so under-developed that transport is at best 'limited' and at worst 'pathetic'?" At times this commodity simply did not exist–at least in the public sector, trains, planes etc–and in Mexico many a journalist must have yearned temporarily for the middle-ages when one could have hired a horse and ridden through the night.

Since the World Cup was resumed after the Second World War, the game has changed

John Radford of Arsenal heads for goal with Mike England and Martin Peters (both Spurs) powerless to stop him.

enormously and so too have the ideas of newspaper proprietors and the companies that publish magazines and books. Back in 1950, for example, when the World Cup was staged in Brazil, the entire British contingent of press-men was immediately recalled when England was eliminated. With England out of the series before the quarter final stage, the World Cup ceased to be news–the customers were no longer interested so why maintain and sustain a representative in Rio?

But in twenty years the customers have changed, albeit ever so slightly. Pelé, Di Stefano and the European Cup have all played a part in this re-appraisal, but the fact is that today when "our" team is eliminated the World Cup goes on being news until after the final. Even then the colour films, full length movies made to be seen months later in cinemas the world over, prove that the World Cup has converted us all. We are interested not only in our team but in the game and the series and it was

(Below) a delighted Alan Birchenall (Crystal Palace) after scoring. (Right) not so happy is Everton goalkeeper Gordon West, after conceding a goal against Chelsea.

due to the inability to provide the necessary transportation facilities for this changed situation that Mexico proved to be an unsuitable choice.

For the majority, those for example who went to see the England games and stayed in Guadalajara until after the quarter finals and moved on via prearranged transport to Mexico City for the last stages, there were no difficulties. But for the newspaper man charged with covering the other groups, for the "neutrals" who attempted to find the *match of the day* and view the competition overall it was a nightmare. A fraction of the experiences of one man will demonstrate:

Mexico City to Leon for the Peru-Morocco game –overnight sleepers fully booked and no reserves of sleeping cars available; planes fully booked and waiting lists. Answer–a chauffeur-driven car, round trip £50.

Interview with Orvar Bergmark, following the Swede's last match against Uruguay in Puebla. Problem: to return "home" at ten p.m. (local time). Next train 02.00 but on local information it was "unreliable". Sometimes it arrives at 5 a.m., it was said–sometimes it doesn't come at all! Answer: taxi back to Mexico City for £20 and problems to find a taxi driver willing to undertake the trip.

To see Didi after the Peru-Brazil quarter final–it would have been Zagallo had it been Brazil who were eliminated–and then return to base. No point even trying to reserve a seat on a plane or a sleeper on the night train (all booked anyway) because one couldn't be sure what time the task would be completed. Alternative: stay the night in Guadalajara and return to Mexico City in the morning; but all available hotel accommodation had been reserved for months. Nothing doing. The outcome: an overnight journey by bus–inexpensive and the way the Mexicans usually travel–but the only seat available was on a bus which went northwest first to Leon before turning south for the capital. Cheap but unpleasant.

By now it should be clear that the task of covering a World Cup is no picnic. Far from being a "holiday" the working journalist returns home after the final practically exhausted.

By contrast, the competitions of 1954, 1958 and 1966 presented none of these headaches. Staged in Switzerland, Sweden and England respectively all three countries provided ample means of communication between the major cities. Without even

A finger-tip save for Arsenal goalkeeper Bob Wilson, one of this year's IFB contributors.

considering the aeroplane, the railways provided fast and usually efficient means of travel with frequent services every day, every year and during a World Cup the railways in these countries have reserves of rolling stock–restaurant cars, sleeping cars etc on which they can draw if demand warrants it.

The Swiss of course–at home in 1954–have been accustomed to the invasion of tourists by the thousand for many years–indeed they thrive on it. A large proportion of the Swiss population is employed in the tourist trade and the stability of the Swiss Franc would pale a little if tourism were to cease for any reason.

In Sweden where the 1958 competition was staged, tourists were far less numerous but the state railways were even then superb. Stockholm to Gothenburg, from one side of the country to the other, in less than an afternoon and FIFA please note, journalists were offered a "go anywhere by rail ticket" valid from June 1 to June 30 valid for 1st and 2nd class for 150 Swedish Crowns, which at 1970 rates of exchange is a mere £12.

As Gordon Banks says elsewhere in this book . . . "the World Cup belongs to everyone. Every country must have the opportunity to show World Football to their own people . . ." but the fact remains that FIFA could do just a little more to supplement the almost impeccable services it provides for the Press. In particular and before allocating the competition to any country they too should note that more and more journalists are flitting around from group to group and ensure that the transportation facilities thus required are available. Banks' point is valid but it is worth noting that even the Russians who inadvisedly ordered their players and officials to return home as soon as they were eliminated, also **left several journalists behind to cover the rest of the World Cup for their readers.** They should of course also have instructed their officials, manager Katchalin, coach Ponomarev and Simonian, manager of Moscow Spartak who "spied" for Katchalin on future opponents in turn, to stay behind and perhaps discover why the USSR failed to reach the semi-finals.

A typical header from Derek Dougan (right) of Wolves. Also pictured are Hugh Curran (centre) and Peter Simpson of Arsenal.

Football, cricket or . . . to be a policeman

by CLYDE BEST
(Bermuda and West Ham)

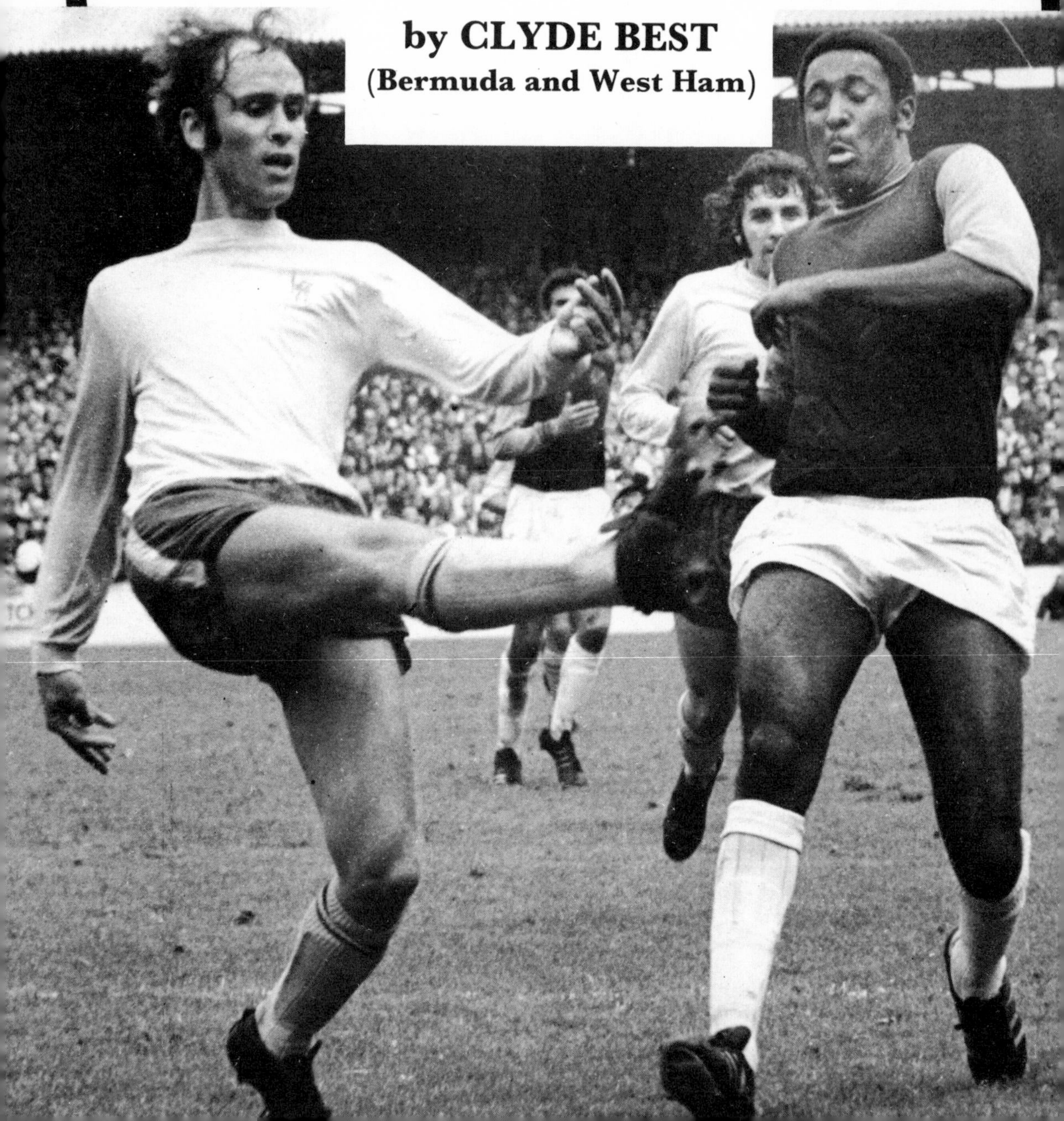

BACK home in Bermuda when I was a youngster I never really thought too much about school or studying. Now that I'm a professional player with West Ham I hope to get down to something serious and study for some kind of qualification, but when I was young I was too busy playing football and cricket.

I liked both games equally well and in Bermuda, where the weather is like an English summer all the year round, I rarely thought about doing anything else. My ambition was to be a professional player–football or cricket–and if I hadn't made it I think I would probably have tried to join the Bermuda police.

Since I joined West Ham I've heard that other clubs were interested in me, but I only heard rumours. The Atlanta Chiefs in the U.S.A. and Arsenal here in England were said to be interested but I left everything to Graham Adams who was my coach at the time. Graham was an Englishman, coaching soccer for my club, the Somerset Cricket Club and I left it all to him. From October to April I played football and from April to September it was cricket–both games for the same club.

When I was around 17 I had a few games for Bermuda representative teams against visiting club sides. I remember playing against a couple of teams from Mexico, and Chelsea too, but before I came to England my biggest games were the two World Cup qualifying matches I played in against the United States. That was back in 1968 and shortly after this Graham Adams told me that he'd arranged for me to go to England for a two-month trial with West Ham.

From then on things happened rapidly. I came, trained and played for West Ham and finally became a professional and I had made it. But more than that I didn't realise at the time just how lucky I was in signing for West Ham for I left all the arrangements to Graham and it was he who arranged it. Now that I'm here I realise only too well that West Ham for me are the best club in the world–I just wouldn't want to go anywhere else.

For one thing, I'm grateful to them for giving me the opportunity to be a professional. But more than that, the club manager Ron Greenwood, to

(Left) Clyde Best of West Ham with Chelsea's John Dempsey. (Right) . . . a smiling Clyde Best, happy to be a member of the set-up at West Ham.

A goal for Liverpool against Everton . . . the scorer being Chris Lawler (centre, background) with Andy Rankin the beaten goalkeeper. On the right are Phil Boersma of Liverpool and John Hurst of Everton.

me, is the best fellow in the world. He is a real gentleman, and he treats me like a gentleman and you cannot ask for more than that from your boss.

Of course, there's a big difference between the game in Bermuda and the professional game here in England. But because of ties going back over the years between the two countries and the fact that many of the coaches in Bermuda are either of British origin or qualified as coaches in England, the game there is played along the same lines.

The first difference that strikes you immediately is, of course, the climate and the effect this has on the playing pitches. In Bermuda you can train and play all the year round on good grass, even though the ground is harder. Overall the training facilities for youngsters in Bermuda are really excellent, in one or two places even better than in England. In this country it's only the comparatively small number of youngsters' who are lucky enough to attract the attention of professional clubs, who can train with the best facilities.

For me, football-wise, the biggest differences were in the speed of the game here in England and the opportunity to learn new skills in training almost every day. And my biggest problems stemmed from the British climate which, of course, affects the playing conditions. I wouldn't say that I dislike the mud, but playing on snow or ice is something else again. On ice and slippery surfaces you just can't reproduce your skills, you can't express yourself as you can on a good surface.

But as a professional player, like it or not, you just have to accept it and do the best you can. It comes to this: I play for West Ham and if the club manager tells me I'm playing then I play and whatever the conditions I do the best I can.

There has been speculation about changing the English season or introducing a mid-winter break and while I think it would be a good thing generally–you can't really play top quality football on bad surfaces on which you find it difficult to stop suddenly or change direction without slipping over–I have two minds about it. I think it would be good for the game as a whole–but I like to be able to spend my summer holiday back in Bermuda and obviously I can't have it both ways.

When I got the chance to play in the first team at West Ham it took me two or three games to adjust to the greater speed of the game but I was lucky enough to have five or six really good players around me and they certainly made it easier for me. Playing with good players around you automatically raises your game.

Tackling in England is quicker and harder, generally the game is rougher and defenders 'play the man' more than in other countries I think. This only applies to one or two teams here, teams whose players have adopted a fully professional attitude and want only to win. Of course results are important but my personal choice would be a balance between playing good football and winning.

To play good football or attractive football but lose is obviously no good–let's face it, a team that loses every week just can't be a good side, so we have to aim for both: a good game and a good result. Ideally, I'd like to play good football all the time and win most of the games. Winning the league and the cup is what it's all about. I don't mind losing now and again though . . . as long as it's not too often . . . and anyway even the top teams get beaten occasionally.

In any case, even if it was possible to win every game I don't think it would be a good thing. It does you good–the individual and the team–to lose now and again for that's the way you learn

Neil Martin (playing for Coventry before his transfer to Nottingham Forest) hooks the ball away from Clyde Best (West Ham).

things, you find out what went wrong and try to learn from your mistakes and failures. And I'm sure it would be a bad thing if you won everything you played for–the league, the cup, the league cup, the World Cup. You win everything and the game losses some of its appeal and in terms of character I think it could spoil people if they always won. In this sense you need to lose now and again to keep you level headed and working hard at training, but as I said earlier . . . not too often. Just enough to keep you in line.

I'm still only 20 now but already I've seen quite a bit of the world, thanks to football, but I find playing against different kinds of teams just as interesting as the travelling. Last year, for example, I played for West Ham against Santos in New York and I was lucky enough to score both our goals. We drew 2–2 and the goals I got made me feel really good–not just because they went in against Santos but for the simple reason that they were my first goals of the season.

But I certainly welcomed the chance to get a close-up view of Pelé–he really is the greatest. It's difficult to say why exactly; others, better educated than I, have tried already but I would say simply that he can do everything, he's the complete player and maybe most important . . . he can do things that no other player in the World can do.

Rather than look back I'd prefer to look forward to all the games I hope to play in future–for West Ham of course. Having already played for Bermuda it's impossible for me to think of international football, playing for England, so my ambitions are inevitably tied in with those of West Ham. And if I can offer a word of advice to youngsters who want to play football and be professionals, set your sights on West Ham because this is where you can learn what the game is all about.

Personally I've been more than happy with West Ham, even though I have been left out of the team now and again. But if I found myself permanently in the reserves I'm sure that I'd think about it very carefully before asking for a transfer because I don't think you could find another club as good as this one.

Crystal Palace right back and captain John Sewell.

Manchester United goalkeeper Alex Stepney, an England international.

LAU VAN RAVENS (FIFA and Holland) says

Referees should not be judged by birth certificates

Referees have come in for a great deal of criticism during recent years and while the general opinion is that refereeing standards are in decline, Holland has earned a growing reputation for producing top class officials. Leo Horn was the first Dutch referee to

Ron Greenwood, a member of the FIFA Technical Committee in Mexico, chats with referee Lau Van Ravens.

become an internationally known figure–requested to control important games all over the World and in my opinion the best referee I've ever seen. But if Mr. Horn was at times a controversial figure, popularity alone is no guide to the ability of an official. The real test is to be in control of a continuous string of important "big-bonus" matches and not only to refrain from booking or sending players off but to see that the games are played in a sportsmanlike manner, not only within the letter of the law but in the right spirit.

To do this requires character, personality, dedication and impartiality as well as an understanding of the laws of the game and the players. Horn had all these qualities and more, and with a growing number of Dutch officials being promoted to the FIFA list, it may be said that it was he who made the break-through to the highest class for referees from Holland.

Carrying on this tradition is Laurens (Lau) Van Ravens who in 1970 was the man I would have named to officiate at any international match which seemed likely to create friction and dissent–and done so with absolute confidence that the game would have passed off without incident.

Eric G. Batty

REFEREES are not born but made, developing over a period of years through experience, and unhappily you cannot cram the understanding that comes from twenty years "in the middle" into a three-year training course. This makes it all the more regrettable that most National Associations have fixed an age-limit at which referees are not exactly forced to retire, but are no longer considered for first class appointments and if they wish to go on refereeing they have to be satisfied to do so at a level below that of the top class professionals.

During a match, the referee might appear to some people to be a special kind of person but, of course, they are just as human and equally liable to make mistakes as anyone else. Their very humanity adds weight to my feeling that you cannot fix a date or an age at which referees pass their peak, for while some people live to be 100 many unfortunate people die in their twenties or even earlier.

Examinations, both physical and mental, and reports from experienced officials who could be appointed to watch and give an up-to-date assessment of a referee's capabilities seem to me to be the only real ways in which anyone can decide whether or not he be invited to carry on at the top level or be

Rinus Israel, a member of the Feyenoord team which won the 1970 European Cup final against Celtic.

Carlos Alberto, skipper of Brazil in the 1970 World Cup series, and a member of the Santos club.

taken off the list. But, if this is too difficult or even judged to be impossible, there must surely be a better method than fixing an arbitrary age at which referees are reckoned to be too old for top class football.

The way things are at the moment, an inexperienced referee would certainly find himself out of his depth if given control of big matches too soon but on the present basis it seems that almost as soon as a referee is judged to be good enough, he is automatically approaching the "retirement" age.

In Mexico last year I was the oldest of the referees in the Leon Group in the 1970 World Cup and at 47, the World Series was to have been the grand finale for me. But, as luck would have it, I was elected the best referee in Holland during the 1969-70 season. After gaining the "Golden Whistle" –my 15 years old daughter Mariane stood in for me when the trophy was presented on Dutch television during the World Cup–the Royal Dutch F.A. announced that my licence was to be extended for one more year.

Of course, I was delighted for football plays an important part in my life and if I do take it seriously and train hard, I'm sure that I'm closer to the average referee rather than an exception. I do everything possible to get myself in good shape and stay that way–sleeping a regular eight hours each night–and never smoke or drink.

I was a player in my younger days–a goalkeeper with SVV and between 1939 and 1941 I was their first team goalkeeper. Then the war disrupted all football and finally, when it was all over, I began to referee in 1948. Seventeen years later I reached my new "goal" . . . promotion to the FIFA list. If anything I train even harder to keep fit for my new role than I did when I was a goalkeeper. Three evenings a week I go out running . . . alone except for my stop watch.

During my time in the game, football has become harder but not, in my opinion, too hard. As long as the individual players discipline themselves the present position seems to me just about right. For referees, as long as they are on their toes it's no more difficult to control a game today than it was ten years ago and the most important thing for referees, in my view, is the famous Law 18. FIFA, of course, gives us only 17 Laws but the unwritten 18th Law is that which we refer to as the one which gives officials "discretionary powers." The secret (if there is one) to being a good referee—apart from understanding the Laws and how to interpret them—lies in not being too hard and not being too easy.

During my 22 years' refereeing in Holland I've sent off only five or six players and at international level none at all . . . though I have cautioned two players in international games. There are differences between officiating in one country and another and referees have to be adaptable, too. For example, I have found that in Holland the players tend to dispute decisions and want to argue more than the English players do. Perhaps this stems from tradition, I don't know, but from my experience British players accept decisions and get on with the game.

One of the matches I most enjoyed was the Scotland-England game at Hampden Park, Glasgow in 1968. The result was a 1-1 draw and I hope the players and spectators enjoyed it as much as I did.

Here, I think, a word of explanation about how referees enjoy games might help. Perhaps satisfaction would be a better word than enjoy. Deep down I have a real love for the game and, having taken part in a really good match, sitting in the dressing room afterwards, reflecting on the last two hours, knowing that no one was injured, no one sent off and that it really was a fine game gives me both satisfaction and pleasure. That, I think, is the closest I can get to what I mean by enjoying a game.

I go to watch football, too, as a spectator and one thing I feel should be emphasised more. Referees should make more use of their linesmen who are, after all, referees themselves. I know the individual referees all have their own way of working but to me I know that if there are any difficulties or critical decisions to be made the only help and advice I can get is from the linesmen.

I believe the three officials should work as a team and if one of the linesmen sees something that he thinks the referee could not or did not see then he should tell him. And, if the incident is serious enough I would never hesitate to send a player off, because in my opinion that's what the linesmen are there for . . . to assist the referee in his attempt to ensure that the game is played according to the Laws. And I learned a long time ago that the referee cannot possibly see everything.

Paul Van Himst, one of Belgium's greatest ever players.

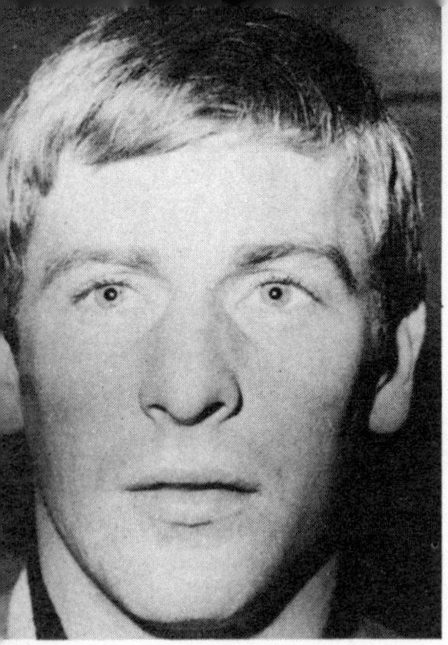

Leon Jeck of Belgium

Georgi Asparoukhov of Bulgaria

Roland Ducke of East German

'ladimar Hrivnak of Czechoslovakia (above) Moshe Romano of Israel (below)

Wilson Piazza of Brazil (above) and Florea Dumitrache of Rumania (below)

Enrico Albertosi of Italy (above) Enrique Borja of Mexico (bel

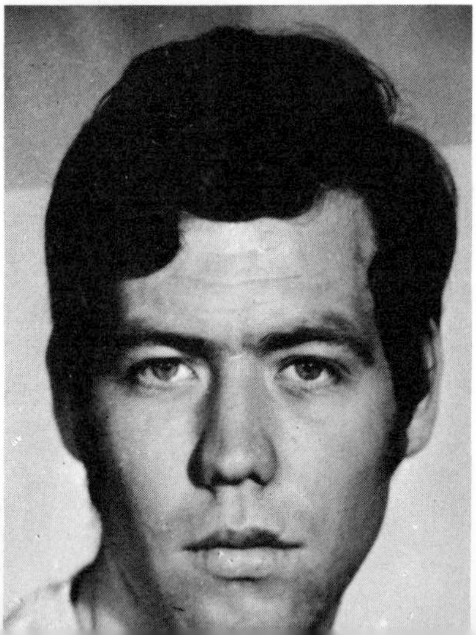

Kunishige Kamamoto
(of Japan)
says

I WAS BORN TOO EARLY

Kunishige Kamamoto, with the Emperor's Cup, won by his club Yanmar Diesel.

ALMOST all sports activities in Japan are organised by factories, schools and universities and if you want to participate in any sport you must either find employment with a large, well organised company or be a student of some kind. Otherwise, and this applies particularly to soccer, it is virtually impossible to get a game at all. Even now not all primary schools (for boys under twelve years) include soccer amongst their activities, though this is changing as soccer becomes more and more popular.

Many of my colleagues in the Japanese national team could not play soccer at all until they entered what we call middle school when they were twelve and this, of course, is a tremendous disadvantage compared with other countries. I myself was very fortunate for while my sports career began with baseball—still the most popular game in Japan, imported from the U.S.A.—I was lucky enough to attend a school where one of the teachers had a great interest in soccer.

This was in Kyoto which is one of our most ancient cities situated in western Japan. I was born there in 1944 and by the time I was 9 or 10 I had become something of a star 'slugger' in schools baseball. Like most of my schoolmates I dreamt of becoming a

Two action shots of Kunishige Kamamoto, Japan's outstanding player.

professional but deep down my real ambition was to travel and see as much of the world as possible. It was around this time that I took up football rather than baseball and it was largely because of my teacher's advice. "Baseball," he told me, "is played only in the U.S.A. If you really want to travel you should play soccer because that is the World game."

Since then I have realised how right he was and in fact I was still in High school when I first travelled abroad with the Japanese Youth team that took part in the 1961 Asian Youth Football Tournament staged that year in Bangkok. I was terribly excited by it all but even before we arrived back in Tokyo after the games, I had already been brought back from the clouds with a real bang. Looking back I can see very clearly that I imagined that being chosen to play for Japan was an end in itself.

The man who made me realise that the Asian Youth Cup was only the beginning was Dettmar Cramer. Mr Cramer came from West Germany at the invitation of the Japanese Football Association in September 1960 with the primary task of preparing the Japanese team for the Olympic Games held in Tokyo in 1964. He travelled all over our country, helping club teams by coaching and introduced European training methods but most of his time was given to preparing all Japanese Representative teams. He was a small, keen-eyed man who had already given me a great deal of encouragement, telling me, for example, that I could win a place in the National team for the Olympic Games.

But, on the way home from Bangkok, Mr Cramer really gave me a dressing down. Loudly and firmly he warned me that I had no reason to be complacent. I remember his exact words as clearly as if this incident had taken place yesterday. "In the Japanese game," he told me, "your height, strength and shooting power are decisive weapons but the level of the game in Japan does not compare favourably with other countries. Even at Asian Youth level you are too slow to turn; too slow to move, too slow to shoot—too slow to beat any opponent at full international level."

After this analysis and criticism by Mr Cramer I was determined to work even harder at the game. He had made me realise that I was like a frog in a tiny well—feeling important but quite ignorant of the whales and sharks that dominate the great oceans of the world.

Yanmar Diesel FC of Osaka, winners of the Emperor's Cup in 1971. Kamamoto is in the centre of the front row.

Three years later when Japan staged the 1964 Olympics, our soccer team beat Argentina 3–2—we scored 5 goals and reached the quarter finals but as Mr Cramer had predicted I was not really ready and didn't score myself. But from then on this relative success in the Olympics had a great impact on the country and the game went through a period of major reconstruction. Until then soccer had been based on regional leagues but from 1965 the first Japanese National league was organised with eight clubs from Tokyo, Nagoya, Osaka, Hiroshima and Kita-Kyushu. At that time I was playing for the team of the University at Waseda and when I graduated in 1967 the game was firmly established and the national league a big success.

I received offers from most of the top teams but finally accepted an offer from the Yanmar Diesel Company because their factory at Osaka is located close to my home town of Kyoto. At that time I had already been voted 'Footballer of the Year' in 1966 but, not forgetting the criticisms of Mr Cramer, I was still not satisfied with my play.

In 1967 Yanmar Diesel FC were fifth in the league out of eight clubs and then suddenly the whole team seemed to lift itself up. Without doubt 1968 was a wonderful year particularly for me. We finished second in the league but won the Emperor's Cup for the first time and I was once more voted 'Player of the Year.' We won the Cup again in 1970 but 1968 was the big year for me personally. First I spent three months as a guest of Saarbrucken FC in West Germany where I really believe my game became much sharper. Then there was the thrill of the 1968 Olympic Games in Mexico when Japan surprised everyone, and I even surprised myself by scoring seven goals to finish top scorer in the competition.

I think that a big part of my success developed from the fact that most of our opponents underestimated our team. It had been clear before our trip to Mexico that whenever we lost the ball, it was the duty of everyone, even the centre forward, to make an immediate effort to regain possession. But in the Olympics our coach surprised me by telling me repeatedly: "That's not your job, always stay well upfield to try and score.".

In this way it was expected that our opponents would tight-mark me—but no one did. In the first game against Nigeria I got a hat trick and even in

Above left) Francis Lee of Manchester City and England. (Above centre) Dennis Smith of Stoke City. (Above right) Roy MacFarland of Derby County and England. (Below left) Steve Kember of Crystal Palace.

Above centre) Mick Jones of Leeds United and England. (Above right) Mick Bailey of Wolverhampton Wanderers and England. Below left) Ray Kennedy of Arsenal. (Below centre) Brian Hall of Liverpool. (Below right) Tony Brown of West Bromwich Albion.

the quarter final against France I was left almost alone. I was lucky enough to score twice in that match—but I think I should have had more. Only in the semi finals against Hungary was I close-marked and we lost decisively by 0–5.

This set-back didn't keep us suppressed for very long because three days later we met the home side, Mexico, in the third place match. With 40,000 people watching—the biggest crowd we'd ever played before—we won 2–0 to get the 3rd place medals and on top of that we also earned the FIFA 'Fair Play' trophy.

Almost at once I began to receive professional offers from clubs in Mexico and several South American countries. But I never had any ambitions beyond Japan though this doesn't mean that I would remain an amateur if professionalism was introduced in Japan. As things are now I have a good job in the administration of Yanmar and we train almost every evening from 5 p.m. for around 90 minutes.

But perhaps the most important thing which keeps me in Japan is the family atmosphere that has grown up in our national team as we prepared for the Olympics in Tokyo and Mexico. More than anything I would like to help Japan win the next series in Munich in 1972 for I really believe we can do it.

From a more personal angle it is a pity that I was born too early. I am sure we will have professional football here within 10 years and maybe then I can earn a living as a coach or manager.

For their last league match of the 1970–71 season, Scottish champions Celtic fielded the team which won the European Cup in 1967. The ex-Champions beat Clyde 6–1.

Watch out for us in 1974

says
TEOFILO
CUBILLAS
the Pelé of Peru

SOON after the World Cup in Mexico, the Peru FA introduced a new regulation under which players could not be transferred to a foreign club until they were at least 25 years old. One or two of our World Cup 22 had already joined clubs in Argentina and Chile and most of us had received offers—as I had myself. For me, and the two colleagues I know best, Baylon and Leon, we were agreed that we should remain in Peru for at least one more attempt to win the World Cup.

This might seem cocky coming from someone as young as I (I'm still only 22) while Baylon and Leon are both around 18 months older than me . . . but there really is a big difference between confidence and being cocky. In a football sense we all three 'grew up' during 1969 and 1970. Looking back I can remember every minor detail precisely yet in some strange way I feel that it all happened to someone else—not me!

To begin with we had all been subjected to the influence of our national team coach, Waldyr Pereira. Didi, as he was known in his playing days, was so full of confidence—it was impossible not to be affected by him. Even after we had lost our first qualifying match 2–1 against Bolivia in La Paz, Didi never wavered for a moment. Outwardly at least he was always calm and somehow he always

managed to find the right words for every different occasion.

For example, in that first game against Bolivia our hard-working wing half Ramon Mifflin had been sent off after protesting to the referee when he disallowed a goal for us. When it was all over, Didi quietly pointed out that we must learn from this experience to control our feelings: "We don't want anyone sent off in the games against Argentina or in the World Cup next year in Mexico," he said.

Didi had been in charge of our preparations for almost a year when we met Argentina, the first time in Lima and won 1–0. The Argentinians played very defensively but were thrown into chaos by a very shrewd touch by Didi. Right winger Baylon wore the number 11 shirt and lined up at the start on the left wing. Then, after only a few moments, he moved over to the right. It was only a minor thing perhaps but the effect this had on the Argentinian defenders was catastrophic!

After our qualification the national squad retired to our training camp at Trujillo for eight weeks. Situated high in the Andes about 300 miles north of Lima it was an ideal spot for intensive physical training at a similar altitude to that of Leon where we would play our opening games in the World Cup proper. But already major problems had developed

(Above) Gerd Muller of West Germany scores against Peru in the Mexico World Cup finals and (Left) Peru trainer Didi.

over the fitness of two regular players—goalkeeper Luis Rubinos and my Alianza team-mate Julio Baylon. As things turned out, Rubinos made a normal recovery following a cartilage operation at the end of 1969 but Baylon never reached a fully-fit state in 1970.

After even the lightest work-out his knee would swell up and every week fluid had to be drawn off. Even then he could not train properly and he began to put on weight so that when the time came to leave for Mexico he was nearly 10 kilos ($1\frac{1}{2}$ stone) overweight.

At his best Baylon could do 100 metres in 11 seconds—equal to 100 yards in less than 10 seconds, but in Mexico he never showed his true form. Without Baylon's power and thrust on the right wing Didi had no alternative but to introduce Hugo Sotil although he was never really a winger at all. Sotil was so talented he could often keep the ball against really determined opposition for as long as a minute, and he liked nothing better than to dribble past his opponents—then letting them catch him so that he could do it again.

When he plays for Deportivo Municipal in Lima there is a regular 20,000 paying just to watch him and only rarely does another club get better crowds. Unfortunately Sotil's talents were so great and unorthodox that while he mesmerised the opposition

The Peru players in training before the start of the 1970 World Cup finals.

West German goalkeeper, Sepp Maier, saves from Alberto Gallardo of Peru.

he also confused his team-mates by holding the ball too long.

However, despite the problems, we qualified for the quarter finals and then got the opponents we had all been waiting for . . . Brazil. Having already disposed of Argentina we saw no reason to fear the Brazilians—though we certainly respected them. Most of the experts who saw this game said it was a fine, evenly balanced match. To me it seemed there was nothing in it between the two teams and late in the second half when we were 2-3 down I personally missed two very good chances to score. One was an absolutely 'open goal'.

If one of those chances had gone in who can say what might have happened? Certainly we gave Brazil a really good run and finally lost by 4–2 and we were in fact the only team that attacked Brazil and in spite of our relative inexperience we certainly could have beaten them.

Now we must look forward to 1974 and already Didi's successor, Marcos Calderon, is reconstructing our team, replacing the players who were over 25 in 1970. If we can retain the backbone of the team until 1974 then I really believe that we will have a chance. To quote Didi's own words: "Real football is attacking football based on 6 or 7 man attacks with team-work more prominent than individual ability even though the players as individuals must be highly skilled."

Skill, team-work and fitness are the essentials though it was not until we had started to play in Mexico that I realised how important the physical preparation is. Only then did we appreciate what Didi had done—forcing us to sweat at Trujillo.

THE YEAR'S INTERNATIONAL FOOTBALL

THE period under review this year includes that of the final stages of the 1970 World Championship won by Brazil in Mexico but it is a matter of fact that no sooner does the whistle blow at the end of the Final match of one World Championship than we—the fans—are being asked to look ahead to the next one—to, in this case, West Germany in 1974 but with, of course, the qualifying competition starting two years earlier.

Obviously the feeling that the present and the future matter more than the past where football is concerned is consolation to all save the winning country but, as we know ourselves from direct experience, it is not confined to the losers. I would be prepared to take on a modest bet that almost concurrent with the earliest articles extolling England's 1966 World Championship triumph there were already others appearing that asked about our chances for 1970—in particular perhaps some that, guided more by knowledge of a player's birth certificate than his unknown ability of four years hence, were busily discarding some of the 1966 heroes!

As it happens, in Europe there is scarcely any break in the round of competitive football at international level with the qualifying competition for the European Football Championship beginning at the end of each World Championship, and the qualifying competition for the next World Championship beginning more or less as that European Football Championship reaches its final stages—a circumstance that has inspired serious discussion as to the possibilities of the European Football Championship, and possibly similar competitions in the other continents, being used additionally as a qualifying competition for the succeeding World Championship.

In a crowded competitive programme for the leading clubs in Europe it does become increasingly difficult for national sides to arrange dates for their competitive matches without conflicting with the natural demands of clubs, engaged in crowded European and domestic competitive programmes, to retain the services of players who are also wanted for the national 'club' squads. It seems likely to me that, possibly for the 1978 World Championship, the continental championships between nations will also be used as qualifying competitions for the world trophy. That is not, however, the position at the moment and most of the team managers of European national teams will have approached the current European Football Championship both with the intention of doing well in that competition and with the need to blood new players with the 1974 World Championship qualifying and, they hope, final stage matches in mind. Not, given the best support from clubs, an easy task, and, with only grudging support from clubs who may feel that they had already made sacrifices for the 1970 World Championship, a difficult one.

Probably the European countries who did well in the 1970 World Championship or, for that matter, all those who qualified for the final stages in Mexico, are the more vulnerable with the countries who failed to get to Mexico eager to topple those who did and so boost their national ego before the 1974 World Championship qualifying competition.

It all adds up to making the European Football Championship of 1972 (when the final stages will be contested) a much more competitive, and important, affair than was the first European Nations Cup for which 17 Associations entered—only fractionally more than half the total of UEFA's affiliated members. The British 'four' were all conspicuous by their absences but it was the Republic of Ireland who played host in Dublin in the first-ever match in the competition on 5 April 1959. The Irish celebrated by beating Czechoslovakia 2–0 but were eliminated on the aggregated score after the second leg which they lost 0–4. The competition was then organised on Cup lines with home and away legs to each tie until the semi-final stage at which point the four survivors took part in a straightforward knockout tournament in the country of one of the four. France were the first host country for the final tournament but were beaten in an exciting, if at times almost ludicrous, semi-final in Paris by Yugoslavia (4–5) whilst in Marseilles the Soviet Union beat Czechoslovakia 3–0. The Soviet Union went on to win the final in Paris on 10 July 1960 by the odd goal in three after extra time.

The Soviet Union also reached the final of the second Nations Cup competition but were themselves beaten 2–1 by Spain playing at home in Madrid on 21 June 1964. There was a much larger entry for this competition with England, Wales and N. Ireland taking part, not to mention Malta and Albania—but not Scotland.

Scotland made their first entry in the third—and the last completed—competition when the European Nations Cup as such was replaced by the European Football *Championship* in which the entering national associations were placed in groups (usually of four nations) to compete on a league basis, with each playing their rivals twice (once home, once away), for the eight quarter-final places. Then the Cup pattern of two-legged ties determined the four semi-finalists.

There were some doubts felt by the English as well as the Scottish FA as to the possibility of competing both in the European Football Championship and in the annual British Home Championship, and UEFA exceptionally agreed that for the first European Football Championship (or *third* 'Nations Cup') the British Home Championship could serve as a qualifying group for the European Championship. The competition got under way in the season following England's 1966 World Championship victory but although England headed their BHC qualifying group and reached the final tournament with home and away quarter-final wins over Spain, they failed to add the European to the World Championship when they lost (1–0) to Yugoslavia in the semi-final. The final stage of the competition took place in Italy and the host country, after 'winning' their semi-final against the Soviet Union on the toss of a disc (the match itself was goalless), won a replayed final against Yugoslavia by two goals to nil in Rome on 10 June 1968.

Since which time Italy, I suppose one could say appropriately, confirmed their European title by reaching the final of the 1970 World Championship. For the benefit of new IFB readers—and old ones who have not completed the blank end page of last year's statistical section, the bare results of the final stage matches of the World Championship have been included, together with details of Brazil's line-ups throughout the year. Generally however the emphasis is on the 1970-72 European Football Championship with special regard paid to some of the group opponents of the home countries. As in the past few years IFBs I have come away from the traditional positional references and attempted to show line-ups more realistically in 4-3-3, or, much less often, *4-2-4 formations but I must, as before, add the cautionary note that these formations need to be treated imaginatively—particularly where substitutions are concerned. GORDON JEFFERY

WORLD CUP 1970

Quarter-Finals

Match A (Mexico City)

U.S.S.R. (Gr. I Winner)	0	Uruguay (Gr. II Runner-up)	1

Match B (Toluca)

Italy (Gr. II Winner)	4	Mexico (Gr. I Runner-up)	1

Match C (Guadalajara)

Brazil (Gr. III Winner)	4	Peru (Gr. IV Runner-up)	2

Match D (Leon)

W. Germany (Gr. IV Winner)	3	England (Gr. III Runner-up)	2

Semi-Finals

Uruguay (Winner Match A)	1
Italy (Winner Match B)	4

Brazil (Winner Match C)	3
W. Germany (Winner Match D)	3

Match to decide 3rd and 4th ratings
(between beaten semi-finalists)

W. Germany	1	Uruguay	0

FINAL

BRAZIL	4	ITALY	1

AUSTRIA

A	8. 4. 70	Yugoslavia (Bajevic)	1	Austria (Redl)	1	— Sarajevo
B	12. 4. 70	Austria (Migas o.g.)	1	Czechoslovakia (Albrecht, Hrdlicka, Adamec)	3	— Vienna
C	30. 4. 70	Brazil (Rivelino)	1	Austria	0	— Rio de Janeiro
D	10. 9. 70	Austria	0	Yugoslavia (Bajevic)	1	— Graz
E	27. 9. 70	Hungary (Vidats)	1	Austria (Redl)	1	— Budapest
F	7. 10. 70	Austria (Kreuz)	1	France	0	— Vienna
G	31. 10. 70	Austria (Parits)	1	Italy (De Sisti, Mazzola)	2	— Vienna (EFC)

	A	B	C	D	E	F	G
Harreither	G	G[1]	—	—	—	—	—
Rettensteiner	—	G[2]	G	—	—	—	G[2]
Fraydl	—	—	—	G	—	—	—
Koncilia	—	—	—	—	G	G	G[1]
Pumm	RB	RB	RB	—	—	—	LB
Demantke	—	—	—	RB	—	RB[2]	—
Clement	—	—	—	—	RB	RB[1]	—
Schmid-Radner	RCB	RCB	RCB	—	LCB	RCB	RB
Sturmberger	LCB	LCB	LCB	RCB	RCB[1]	LCB	RCB
W. Huberts	LB	LB	LB	—	—	—	—
Strasser	—	—	—	LB	—	—	—
Fak	—	—	—	—	LB	LB	—
Geyer	RH	RH	—	RH	RH	—	—
Krieger	CH	CH	—	LCB	RCB[2]	RH[2]	—
N. Hof	—	—	CH	LH[1]	RF	CH	LCB
Hickersberger	—	LH[2]	—	CH	CH	RH[1]	CH
Ettmayer	LH	LH[1]	RH	LH[2]	LH[2]	LH[2]	LH
Huberts	—	—	LH	—	—	—	—
Starek	—	—	—	—	LH[1]	LH[1]	RH
Pirkner	RF	RF[1]	—	LF	—	—	—
Kreuz	—	RF[2]	CF	CF	CF	CF	CF
Parits	CF	CF	RF	RF	—	RF	RF
Redl	LF	LF	LF	—	LF	LF	LF

BELGIUM

A	3. 6. 70	Belgium (Van Moer 2, Lambert)	3	El Salvador	0	— Mexico City (WC)
B	6. 6. 70	U.S.S.R. (Bishovets 2, Asatiani, Khmelnitsky)	4	Belgium (Lambert)	1	— Mexico City (WC)
C	11. 6. 70	Mexico (Pena)	1	Belgium	0	— Mexico City (WC)
D	15. 11. 70	Belgium (Van Moer)	1	France (Molitor 2)	2	— Brussels
E	25. 11. 70	Belgium (Devrindt 2)	2	Denmark	0	— Bruges (EFC)
F	3. 2. 71	Belgium (McKinnon o.g., Van Himst 2)	3	Scotland	0	— Liege (EFC)
G	17. 2. 71	Belgium (Lambert 2, Denul)	3	Portugal	0	— Brussels (EFC)

	A	B	C	D	E	F	*G
Piot	G	G	G	G	G	G	G
Heylens	RB	RB	RB	—	RB	RB	RB
Bastyns	—	—	—	RB	—	—	—
Dewalque	RCB	RCB	RCB	RCB	RCB	RCB	RCB
Jeck	—	LCB	LCB	LCB	LCB	—	—

Plaskie	—	—	—	—	—	LCB	LCB
Thissen	LB	LB	LB	LB	LB	LB	LB
Van Moer	RH	RH	RH	RH	RH[1]	RH	RH
Verheyen	—	—	—	—	RH[2]	—	—
Dockx	LCB	CH	CH	LH	—	—	—
Van Den Daele	—	—	—	CH	CH	CH	LH
Semmeling	LH	LH	RF	RF[1]	—	RF	OR[1]
Polleunis	RF[2]	—	LH[1]	—	—	—	—
Carteus	—	—	—	CF	LH	—	—
Lambert	RF[1]	RF	—	—	LF	—	RCF
Thio	—	—	—	RF[2]	RF	—	OR[2]
Devrindt	CF	—	LH[2]	—	CF	—	—
Van Himst	CH	CF	CF	—	—	CF	LCF
Puis	LF	LF	LF	—	—	—	—
Teugels	—	—	—	LF	—	—	—
Denul	—	—	—	—	—	LF	OL
Depireux	—	—	—	—	—	LH	—

BRAZIL

A	4. 3. 70	Brazil	0	Argentina (Mas, Conigliaro)	2	— Porto Alegre
B	8. 3. 70	Brazil (Jairzinho, Pelé)	2	Argentina (Brindisi)	1	— Rio
C	22. 3. 70	Brazil (Pelé 2, Gerson, Roberto 2)	5	Chile	0	— Sao Paulo
D	26. 3. 70	Brazil (Carlos Alberto, Rivelino)	2	Chile (Gerson o.g.)	1	— Rio
E	12. 4. 70	Brazil	0	Paraguay	0	— Rio
F	29. 4. 70	Brazil (Rivelino)	1	Austria	0	— Rio
G	3. 6. 70	Brazil (Rivelino, Pelé, Jairzinho 2)	4	Czechoslovakia (Petras)	1	— Guadalajara (WC)
H	7. 6. 70	Brazil (Jairzinho)	1	England	0	— Guadalajara (WC)
I	10. 6. 70	Brazil (Pelé 2, Jairzinho)	3	Rumania (Dumitrache, Dembrowski)	2	— Guadalajara (WC)
J	14. 6. 70	Brazil (Rivelino, Tostao 2, Jairzinho)	4	Peru (Gallardo, Cubillas)	2	— Guadalajara (WC)
K	17. 6. 70	Brazil (Clodoaldo, Jairzinho, Rivelino)	3	Uruguay (Cubilla)	1	— Guadalajara (WC)
L	21. 6. 70	Brazil (Pelé, Gerson, Jairzinho, Carlos Alberto)	4	Italy (Boninsegna)	1	— Mexico City (WC FINAL)
M	30. 9. 70	Brazil (Tostao, Jairzinho)	2	Mexico (Valdivia)	1	— Rio
N	4. 10. 70	Chile (Messen)	1	Brazil (Roberto 2, Pelé, Jairzinho, Paulo Cesar)	5	— Santiago

	*A	*B	*C	*D	*E	*F	G	H	I	J	K	L	M	N
Ado	G	—	—	—	—	—	—	—	—	—	—	—	G[2]	—
Leao	—	G	—	—	—	—	—	—	—	—	—	—	—	—
Felix	—	—	G	G	G	G	G	G	G	G	G	G	G[1]	G
Carlos Alberto	RB	RB	RB	RB	RB	RB	RB	RB	RB	RB	RB	RB	RB	RB
Baldochi	RCB	—	—	—	—	—	—	—	—	—	—	—	—	—
Brito	—	RCB	RCB	RCB	RCB	RCB	RCB	RCB	RCB	RCB	RCB	RCB	RCB	RCB
Fontana	LCB	LCB	—	—	LCB	—	—	—	LH	—	—	—	—	—
Joel	—	—	LCB	LCB	—	—	—	—	—	—	—	—	—	LCB
Marco Antonio	LB	LB	LB	LB	LB	LB	—	—	LB[2]	LB	—	—	—	—
Everaldo	—	—	—	—	—	—	LB	LB	LB[1]	—	LB	LB	LB	LB
Piazza	RH[1]	RH	—	—	—	LCB	LCB	LCB	LCB	LCB	LCB	LCB	LCB	—
Ze Carlos	RH[2]	—	—	—	—	—	—	—	—	—	—	—	—	—
Clodoaldo	—	—	RH[1]	RH	RH	RH	RH	RH	RH[1]	RH	RH	RH	CH	—
Gerson	LH	LH	LH	LH	LH	LH	LH[1]	—	—	LH[1]	LH	LH	LH[1]	—

Paulo Cesar	—	—	OL	OL[1]	OL	—	LH[2]	LH	LF	LH[2]	—	—	LH[2]	LH
Jairzinho	OR	OR	OR	OR	—	OR[2]	RF	RF	RF	RF	RF[1]	RF	RF	RF
Rogerio	—	—	—	—	OR	OR[1]	—	—	—	—	—	—	—	—
Pelé	RCF	RCF	LCF	RCF	LCF	LCF	CH	CH	CH	CH	CH	CH	LF	LF
Dirceu Lopes	LCF	LCF	RH[2]	—	—	—	—	—	—	—	—	—	—	—
Roberto	—	—	RCF	LCF	—	—	—	CF[2]	—	—	RF[2]	—	—	CF
Tostao	—	—	—	—	—	RCF[1]	CF	CF[1]	CF	CF	CF	CF	CF	—
Dos Santos	—	—	—	—	RCF	RCF[2]	—	—	—	—	—	—	—	RH
Ney	—	—	—	—	—	—	—	—	—	—	—	—	—	CH
Edu	OL	OL	—	—	—	—	—	—	RH[2]	—	—	—	—	—
Rivelino	—	—	—	OL[2]	—	OL	LF	LF	—	LF	LF	LF	RH	—

CZECHOSLOVAKIA

A	12. 4. 70	Austria (Migas o.g.)	1	Czechoslovakia (Albrecht, Hrdlicka, Adamec)	3	— Vienna
B	10. 5. 70	Luxembourg	0	Czechoslovakia (Jurkanin)	1	— Luxembourg
C	14. 5. 70	Norway	0	Czechoslovakia (Olafsen o.g., Adamec)	2	— Oslo
D	3. 6. 70	Brazil (Rivelino, Pelé, Jairzinho 2)	4	Czechoslovakia (Petras)	1	— Guadalajara (WC)
E	6. 6. 70	Rumania (Neagu, Dumitrache)	2	Czechoslovakia (Petras)	1	— Guadalajara (WC)
F	11. 6. 70	England (Clarke)	1	Czechoslovakia	0	— Guadalajara (WC)
G	5. 9. 70	France (Gondet, Loubet, Bosquier)	3	Czechoslovakia	0	— Nice
H	7. 10. 70	Czechoslovakia (Albrecht)	1	Finland (Paatelainen)	1	— Prague (EFC)
I	25. 10. 70	Czechoslovakia (Stratil 2)	2	Poland (Kozerski, Blaut)	2	— Prague

	*A	B	C	D	E	F	G	*H	I
Viktor	G	G	G[1]	G	—	G	G[1]	—	—
Vencel	—	—	G[2]	—	G	—	G[2]	—	—
Schmucker	—	—	—	—	—	—	—	G	—
Kramerius	—	—	—	—	—	—	—	—	G[1]
Sedlacek	—	—	—	—	—	—	—	—	G[2]
Dobias	RB	RB	RB	RB	RB	RB	RB	—	—
Vecerek	—	—	—	—	—	—	—	RB	RB
Hrivnak	RCB	RCB	—	—	—	RCB	—	—	—
Horvath	—	LCB	RCB	RCB	RCB	—	—	—	—
Bomba	—	—	—	—	—	—	—	RCB	—
Majernik	—	—	—	—	—	—	—	—	RCB
Migas	LCB	—	LCB	LCB	LCB	LCB	RCB	—	—
J. Novak	—	—	—	—	—	—	LCB	—	—
Desiatnik	—	—	—	—	—	—	—	LCB[1]	—
Urban	—	—	—	—	—	—	—	LCB[2]	LCB
Hagara	LB	—	—	LB	—	LB	LB	—	—
Zlocha	—	LB	LB	—	LB	—	—	—	—
Mutkovic	—	—	—	—	—	—	—	LB	LB
Hrdlicka	RH	RH	RH[1]	RH[1]	—	—	RH[1]	—	—
Pollak	—	CF[2]	RH[2]	—	—	RH	—	—	—
Mojzis	—	—	—	—	—	—	—	RH	—
Petrovic	—	—	—	—	—	—	—	—	RH
Kvasnak	—	CH	—	RH[2]	RH	—	—	—	—
Jurkanin	RCF	LH[1]	CH	—	CH[1]	—	RH[2]	—	—
Adamec	LCF	CF[1]	CF[2]	CH	CH[2]	CH	—	—	—
Geleta	—	—	—	—	—	—	CH	—	—
Bartovic	—	—	—	—	—	—	—	LH	CH[1]
Kuna	LH	LH[2]	LH	LH	LH	LH	LH	—	—
Vrana	—	—	—	—	—	—	—	—	LH
B. Vesely	OR[1]	RF[2]	RF	RF[2]	RF	—	—	—	—
F. Vesely	OR[2]	RF[1]	—	RF[1]	LF[2]	RF	RF	—	—
Strunc	—	—	—	—	—	—	—	OR	RF

Jokl	—	—	CF[1]	LF	LF[1]	LF[2]	—	—	—
Petras	—	—	—	CF	CF	CF	LF[1]	—	—
Szikora	—	—	—	—	—	—	CF	—	—
Nagy	—	—	—	—	—	—	—	RCF[1]	CF[1]
Bicovsky	—	—	—	—	—	—	—	—	CF[2]
Albrecht	OL	LF[1]	—	—	—	—	LF[2]	OL	CH[2]
Jan Capkovic	—	LF[2]	LF	—	—	LF[1]	—	—	—
Stratil	—	—	—	—	—	—	—	LCF	LF
Hoholko	—	—	—	—	—	—	—	RCF[2]	—

ENGLAND

A	18. 4. 70	Wales (Krzywicki)	1	England (Lee)	1	Cardiff (BHC)
B	21. 4. 70	England (Peters, Hurst, R. Charlton)	3	N. Ireland (Best)	1	Wembley (BHC)
C	25. 4. 70	Scotland	0	England	0	Glasgow (BHC)
D	20. 5. 70	Colombia	0	England (Peters 2, R. Charlton, Ball)	4	Bogota
E	23. 5. 70	Ecuador	0	England (Lee, Kidd)	2	Quito
F	2. 6. 70	England (Hurst)	1	Rumania	0	Guadalajara (WC)
G	7. 6. 70	Brazil (Jairzinho)	1	England	0	Guadalajara (WC)
H	11. 6. 70	England (Clarke)	1	Czechoslovakia	0	Guadalajara (WC)
I	14. 6. 70	W. Germany (Beckenbauer, Seeler, Muller)	3	England (Mullery, Peters)	2	Leon (WC)
J	25. 11. 70	England (Lee, Peters, Clarke)	3	East Germany (Vogel)	1	Wembley
K	3. 2. 71	Malta	0	England (Peters)	1	Valetta (EFC)

	A	B	C	D	E	F	G	H	I	J	K
Banks	G	G	G	G	G	G	G	G	—	—	G
Bonetti	—	—	—	—	—	—	—	—	G	—	—
Shilton	—	—	—	—	—	—	—	—	—	G	—
K. Newton	—	RB[1]	RB	RB	RB	RB[1]	—	RB	RB	—	—
Hughes	RB	LB	LB	—	—	—	—	—	—	RB	LB
Reaney	—	—	—	—	—	—	—	—	—	—	RB
Labone	RCB	—	RCB	RCB	RCB	RCB	RCB	—	RCB	—	—
J. Charlton	—	—	—	—	—	—	—	RCB	—	—	—
Stiles	—	RCB	RH	—	—	—	—	—	—	—	—
Sadler	—	—	—	—	—	—	—	—	—	RCB	—
McFarland	—	—	—	—	—	—	—	—	—	—	RCB
Moore	LCB	LCB	LCB	LCB	LCB	LCB	LCB	LCB	LCB	LCB	—
Hunter	—	—	—	—	—	—	—	—	LH[2]	—	LCB
Wright	LB	—	—	—	—	RB[2]	RB	—	—	—	—
Cooper	—	—	—	LB	LB	LB	LB	LB	LB	LB	—
Mullery	RH	RH	RF[2]	RH	RH	RH	RH	RH	RH	RH	RH
Ball	CH	—	CH	CH	CH	CH	CH	CH[2]	CH	CH	CH
Coates	—	CH	—	—	—	—	—	—	—	—	—
Peters	LH	LH	LH	LH	LH	LH	LH	LH	LH[1]	LH	RF
Harvey	—	—	—	—	—	—	—	—	—	—	LH
Lee	RF	—	—	RF	RF[1]	RF[1]	RF[1]	—	RF	RF	—
Bell	—	RB[2]	—	—	—	—	CF[2]	RF	CF[2]	—	—
Kidd	—	RF	—	—	RF[2]	—	—	—	—	—	—
Thompson	—	—	RF[1]	—	—	—	—	—	—	—	—
Osgood	—	—	—	—	—	RF[2]	—	CF[2]	—	—	—
R. Charlton	CF	CF	—	CF	CF	CF	CF[1]	CH[1]	CF[1]	—	—
Astle	—	—	CF	—	—	—	RF[2]	CF[1]	—	—	—
Royle	—	—	—	—	—	—	—	—	—	—	CF
Hurst	LF	LF	LF	LF	LF	LF	LF	—	LF	CF	—
Clarke	—	—	—	—	—	—	—	LF	—	LF	—
Chivers	—	—	—	—	—	—	—	—	—	—	LF

WEST GERMANY

A	11. 2. 70	Spain (Arieta 2)	2	West Germany	0	Seville
B	8. 4. 70	West Germany (Overath)	1	Rumania (Neagu)	1	Stuttgart
C	9. 5. 70	West Germany (Seeler, Lohr)	2	Rep. of Ireland (Mulligan)	1	W. Berlin
D	13. 5. 70	West Germany (Seeler)	1	Yugoslavia	0	Hanover
E	3. 6. 70	West Germany (Seeler, Muller)	2	Morocco (Houmane)	1	Leon (WC)
F	7. 6. 70	West Germany (Libuda, Seeler, Muller 3)	5	Bulgaria (Nikodimov, Kolev)	2	Leon (WC)
G	10. 6. 70	West Germany (Muller 3)	3	Peru (Cubillas)	1	Leon (WC)
H	14. 6. 70	West Germany (Beckenbauer, Seeler, Muller)	3	England (Mullery, Peters)	2	Leon (WC)
I	17. 6. 70	West Germany (Schnellinger, Muller 2)	3	Italy (Boninsegna, Riva, Burgnich, Rivera)	4	Mexico City (WC)
J	20. 6. 70	West Germany (Overath)	1	Uruguay	0	Mexico City (WC)
K	9. 9. 70	West Germany (Sieloff, Muller 2)	3	Hungary (Fazekas)	1	Nuremberg
L	17. 10. 70	West Germany (Muller)	1	Turkey (Kamarun)	1	Cologne (EFC)
M	18. 11. 70	Yugoslavia (Bukal, Dzajic)	2	West Germany	0	Zagreb
N	22. 11. 70	Greece (Youtsos)	1	West Germany (Netzer, Grabowski, Beckenbauer)	3	Athens
O	17. 2. 71	Albania	0	West Germany (Muller)	1	Tirana (EFC)

	*A	B	*C	*D	E	*F	*G	*H	*I	*J	*K	L	M	N	*O
Manglitz	G	—	—	G	—	—	—	—	—	—	—	—	—	—	—
Maier	—	G	—	—	G	G	G	G	G	—	G	G	G	—	G
Wolter	—	—	G	—	—	—	—	—	—	G	—	—	—	—	—
Gross	—	—	—	—	—	—	—	—	—	—	—	—	—	G	—
Vogts	RB	RB	RB	RB	RB	RB	RB	RB	RB	RB	RB	RB	RB	RB	RB
Schulz	RCB	—	RCB	—	RCB	—	—	LCB[2]	LCB	—	—	—	—	—	—
Sieloff	—	RCB[2]	—	—	—	—	—	—	—	—	RCB	RCB[1]	—	RCB	—
Weber	LCB	RCB[1]	LCB	—	—	RH[2]	—	—	—	—	LCB	LCB	RCB	—	LCB
Hottges	—	LCB	—	LB	LCB[1]	LCB	LCB[1]	LCB[1]	—	RH	LB	LB	LB	LB	—
Fichtel	—	—	—	LCB	LB	LB	LB	LB	—	LCB	LH	CH	—	—	—
Bella	—	—	—	—	—	—	—	—	—	—	—	—	—	LCB	LB[2]
Schnellinger	LB	LB	—	RCB	—	RCB	RCB	RCB	RCB	RCB[1]	—	—	—	—	RCB
Patzke	—	—	LB	—	—	—	LCB[2]	—	LB[1]	LB	—	—	—	—	LB[1]
Haller	RH	CH[1]	—	—	RH[1]	—	—	—	—	—	—	—	—	—	—
Flohe	—	—	—	—	—	—	—	—	—	—	—	—	—	CH[2]	—
Beckenbauer	—	RH	RH	RH	CH	RH[1]	RH	RH	RH	—	RH	RH	LCB	RH	RH
Lorenz	—	CH[2]	—	—	—	—	—	—	—	RCB[2]	—	—	—	—	—
Netzer	LH	—	—	—	—	—	—	—	—	—	—	—	CH	CH[1]	RCF
Overath	—	LH	LH[1]	LH	LH	LH	LH	LH	LH	LH	—	LH	LH	LH[1]	LH
Libuda	OR	—	—	OR	—	OR	OR[1]	OR[1]	OL[2]	OR[1]	OL[2]	RF	RF	RF	—
Held	—	—	LH[2]	—	RF	—	—	—	LB[2]	OL	—	—	LF[1]	—	—
Dietrich	—	—	OR[2]	—	—	—	—	—	—	—	—	—	—	—	—
Muller	RCF	CF	LCF	LCF	CF	LCF	LCF	LCF	LCF	LCF	LCF	CF	—	—	LCF
Heynckes	—	—	—	—	—	—	—	—	—	—	—	RCB[2]	CF	CF	OL
Seeler	LCF	—	RCF	RCF	LF	RCF	RCF	RCF	RCF	RCF	RCF	—	—	—	—
Grabowski	OL	RF	OR[1]	—	RH[2]	OL[2]	OR[2]	OR[2]	OR	—	OR	LF	LF[2]	LF	OR
Maas	—	LF[1]	—	—	—	—	—	—	—	—	—	—	—	—	—
Roth	—	LF[2]	—	—	—	—	—	—	—	—	—	—	RH	LH[2]	—
Lohr	—	—	OL	OL	LCB[2]	OL[1]	OL	OL	OL[1]	OR[2]	OL[1]	—	—	—	—

NORTHERN IRELAND

A	18. 4. 70	N. Ireland	o	Scotland (O'Hare)	1	— Belfast (BHC)
B	21. 4. 70	England (Peters, Hurst, R. Charlton)	3	N. Ireland (Best)	1	— Wembley (BHC)
C	25. 4. 70	Wales (Rees)	1	N. Ireland	o	— Swansea (BHC)
D	11. 11. 70	Spain (Rexach, Pirri, Luis)	3	N. Ireland	o	— Seville (EFC)
E	3. 2. 71	Cyprus	o	N. Ireland (Nicholson, Dougan, Best)	3	— Nicosia (EFC)

	A	B	C	D	E
Jennings	G	G	—	—	G
McFaul	—	—	G	G	—
Craig	RB	RB	RB	RB	RB
Todd	RCB[1]	—	—	CF[2]	RCB
O'Kane	RCB[2]	RCB	RCB	RCB	—
Neill	LCB	LCB	LCB	LCB	LCB
Clements	LB	LB	LH	LF	—
Nelson	—	LH[2]	LB	LB	LB
Nicholson	RH	RH	RH	—	RH
Jackson	—	—	—	RH	—
Lutton	CH	LH[1]	—	—	—

	A	B	C	D	E
McMordie	LH	CH	CH	—	CH
Hunter	—	—	—	—	I H
Sloan	—	—	—	CH	—
Harkin	—	—	—	LH	—
Campbell	RF[1]	—	RF[1]	—	—
Dickson	RF[2]	—	CF	—	—
Best	LF	RF	LF	RF	LF
Hamilton	—	—	—	—	RF
O'Doherty	—	LF[1]	RF[2]	—	—
Dougan	CF	CF	—	CF[1]	CF
Cowan	—	LF[2]	—	—	—

REPUBLIC OF IRELAND

A	6. 5. 70	Poland (Kozerski, Szoltysik)	2	Rep. of Ireland (Givens)	1	— Poznan
B	9. 5. 70	West Germany (Seeler, Lohr)	2	Rep. of Ireland (Mulligan)	1	— Hanover
C	23. 9. 70	Rep. of Ireland	o	Poland (Stachurski, Szoltysik)	2	— Dublin
D	14. 10. 70	Rep. of Ireland (Carroll)	1	Sweden (Brzokopil)	1	— Dublin (EFC)
E	28. 10. 70	Sweden (Turesson)	1	Rep. of Ireland	o	— Stockholm (EFC)
F	8. 12. 70	Italy (De Sisti, Prati, Boninsegna)	3	Rep. of Ireland	o	— Florence (EFC)

	A	B	C	D	E	F
Kelly	G	G	G[1]	G	G	G
Kearns	—	—	G[2]	—	—	—
Kinnear	RB	—	—	RB[2]	—	—
Brennan	CH[2]	RB	RB	—	RB	RB
Carroll	LCB	LB	—	RB[1]	—	—
Hand	RCB	LCB	LCB	—	—	—
Dempsey	—	RCB	RCB	RCB	RCB	RCB
Byrne	LB	LH	LB	LCB	LCB	LCB
Dunne	—	—	—	LB	—	—
Dunning	—	—	—	—	LB	LB
Mulligan	RH	CH	CH	LH	—	—
Giles	LH	RH	—	—	—	—

	A	B	C	D	E	F
Dunphy	CH[1]	RF[2]	RH	CH	CH	RH[1]
Lawlor	—	—	LH[1]	RH	LH	RH[2]
Finucane	—	—	—	—	RH	LH
Connelly	—	—	LH[2]	—	—	—
Conway	RF[1]	RF[1]	—	—	—	—
Treacey	RF[2]	LF[2]	CF	LF[2]	LF	LF
Heighway	—	—	LF[1]	RF	RF	—
Conroy	LF	CF	RF	CF	CF	RF
Givens	CF	LF[1]	—	LF[1]	—	CF
Hall	—	—	LF[2]	—	—	—
Rogers	—	—	—	—	—	CH

ITALY

A	22. 2. 70	Spain (Amancio, Salvadore o.g.)	2	Italy (Anastasi, Riva)	2	— Madrid
B	10. 5. 70	Portugal (Humberto)	1	Italy (Riva 2)	2	— Lisbon
C	3. 6. 70	Italy (Domenghini)	1	Sweden	o	— Toluca (WC)
D	6. 6. 70	Italy	o	Uruguay	o	— Puebla (WC)

E	11. 6. 70	Italy	0	Israel	0	Toluca (WC)
F	14. 6. 70	Italy (Domenghini, Riva 2, Rivera)	4	Mexico (Gonzalez)	1	Toluca (WC)
G	17. 6. 70	Italy (Boninsegna, Burgnich, Riva, Rivera)	4	West Germany (Schnellinger, Muller 2)	3	Mexico City (WC)
H	21. 6. 70	Italy (Boninsegna)	1	Brazil (Pelé, Gerson, Jairzinho, Carlos Alberto)	4	Mexico City (WC FINAL)
I	17. 10. 70	Switzerland (Blattler)	1	Italy (Mazzola)	1	Berne
J	31. 10. 70	Austria (Parits)	1	Italy (De Sisti, Mazzola)	2	Vienna (EFC)
K	8. 12. 70	Italy (De Sisti, Prati, Boninsegna)	3	Rep. of Ireland	0	Florence (EFC)
L	20. 2. 71	Italy (De Sisti)	1	Spain (Pirri, Uriarte)	2	Cagliari

	A	B	C	D	E	F	G	H	I	J	K	L
Zoff	G	—	—	—	—	—	—	—	G^{2}	—	—	G
Albertosi	—	G	G	G	G	G	G	G	G^{1}	G	G	—
Burgnich	RB	RB	RB	RB	RB	RB	RB	RB	—	RB	RB	RB^{1}
Ferrante	—	LCB	—	—	—	—	—	—	RH^{2}	—	—	RB^{2}
Puia	RCB	RCB^{1}	—	—	—	—	—	—	—	—	—	—
Cera	RH	—	RCB	RCB	RCB	RCB	RCB	RCB	RB	RCB	RCB	—
Poletti	—	—	—	—	—	—	LCB^{2}	—	RCB	—	—	—
Bet	—	—	—	—	—	—	—	—	—	—	—	RCB
Salvadore	LCB	—	—	—	—	—	—	—	—	—	—	—
Niccolai	—	RCB^{2}	LCB	—	—	—	—	—	LCB	—	—	—
Rosato	—	—	—	LCB	LCB	LCB	LCB^{1}	LCB	—	LCB	LCB	LCB
Facchetti	LB	LB	LB	LB	LB	LB	LB	LB	LB	LB	LB	LB
De Sisti	CH	RH	RH	RH	RH	RH	RH	RH	LH	LH	LH	LH
Bertini	—	LH	LH	LH	LH	LH	LH	LH^{1}	—	RH	RH	RH
Rivera	LH	CH	—	—	RF^{2}	CH^{2}	CH^{2}	CF^{2}	—	CH	—	CH
Mazzola	—	CF^{1}	CH	CH	CH	CH^{1}	CH^{1}	CH	CH	CF	CH	RF
Juliano	—	—	—	—	—	—	—	LH^{2}	RH^{1}	—	—	—
Domenghini	RF	RF	RF	RF^{1}	RF^{1}	RF	RF	RF	RF	RF	RF	—
Furino	—	—	—	RF^{2}	—	—	—	—	—	—	—	—
Anastasi	CF	CF^{2}	—	—	—	—	—	—	—	—	—	—
Boninsegna	—	—	CF	CF	CF	CF	CF	CF^{1}	—	—	CF	CF
Gori	—	—	—	—	—	—	—	—	CF	LF^{2}	—	—
Riva	LF	LF	LF	LF	LF	LF	LF	LF	LF	LF^{1}	—	—
Prati	—	—	—	—	—	—	—	—	—	—	LF	LF

PORTUGAL

A	10. 5. 70	Portugal (Humberto)	1	Italy (Riva 2)	2	Lisbon
B	14. 10. 70	Denmark	0	Portugal (Joao Jacinto)	1	Copenhagen (EFC)
C	17. 2. 71	Belgium (Lambert 2, Denul)	3	Portugal	0	Brussels (EFC)

	A	B	C
Damas	G	G	G
Pedro Gomez	RB	RB	—
Da Silva	—	—	RB^{1}
Rebello	—	—	RB^{2}
Humberto	RCB	RCB	RCB
Jose Carlos	LCB	LCB	—
Rolando	—	—	LCB
Hilario	LB	LB	LB
Rui Rodriguez	RH^{1}	—	LH^{1}
Peres	LH	RH	CH
Pavao	—	—	RH
Martime	RH^{2}	CH^{2}	—

	A	B	C
Graca	CH	LH^{2}	—
Jose Maria	—	CH^{1}	—
Guerreiro	—	—	LH^{2}
Nelson	RF^{1}	—	—
Dinis	RF^{2}	—	—
Jorge	—	RF	—
Baptista	—	—	RF
Torres	CF	—	—
Eusebio	—	CF	CF
Simeos	LF	LH^{1}	LF
Joao Jacinto	—	LF	—

RUMANIA

A	9. 2. 70	Peru (Cubilla)	1	Rumania (Lucescu)	1	Lima
B	8. 4. 70	West Germany (Overath)	1	Rumania (Neagu)	1	Stuttgart
C	28. 4. 70	France (Loubet, Djorkaeff)	2	Rumania	0	Reims
D	6. 5. 70	Rumania	0	Yugoslavia	0	Bucharest
E	2. 6. 70	England (Hurst)	1	Rumania	0	Guadalajara (WC)
F	6. 6. 70	Rumania (Neagu, Dumitrache)	2	Czechoslovakia (Petras)	1	Guadalajara (WC)
G	10. 6. 70	Brazil (Pelé 2, Jairzinho)	3	Rumania (Dumitrache, Dembrowski)	2	Guadalajara (WC)
H	11. 10. 70	Rumania (Dumitrache 2, Nunweiler)	3	Finland	0	Bucharest (EFC)
I	11. 11. 70	Wales	0	Rumania	0	Cardiff (EFC)
J	2. 12. 70	Netherlands (Cruyff 2)	2	Rumania	0	Amsterdam

	*A	*B	*C	D	E	F	G	*H	I	J
Raducanu	G	G	G^{1}	—	—	—	G^{2}	G	G	G
Adamache	—	—	G^{2}	G	G	G	G^{1}	—	—	—
Satmareanu	RB	RB	RB	RB	RB	RB	RB	RB	RB	RB
Halmageanu	RCB	—	—	—	—	—	—	—	RCB^{2}	LH^{1}
Lupescu	—	RCB	RCB	—	RCB	LCB	LCB	LCB	LCB	LCB
Dan Coe	—	—	—	RCB	—	—	—	—	—	—
Dinu	LCB	LCB	LCB	LCB	LCB	RCB	RCB	RCB	RCB^{1}	—
Mocanu	LB	LB	LB	LB	LB	LB	LB	—	LB	LB
Vigu	—	—	—	—	—	—	—	LB	—	—
Nunweiler	RH	RCF	RH	LH	RH	RH	RH	LH	CH	CH
Ghergeli	—	RH^{2}	—	—	—	LH^{2}	—	—	—	—
Dumitru	LH	LH	LH^{1}	CH	CH	LH^{1}	LH	RH	RH	RCB
Pescaru	—	—	LH^{2}	—	—	—	—	—	—	—
Anca	—	—	—	—	—	—	—	—	—	LH^{2}
Dembrowski	—	OL^{2}	—	RH	RH	RF	RF	—	—	RH^{1}
Neagu	OR	OR	OR	RF	RF^{2}	CH	CH	OR^{1}	RF	—
Dobrin	RCF	RH^{1}	RCF^{2}	CF	—	—	—	RCF	LH	LF
Tataru	—	—	—	—	RF^{1}	LF^{2}	CF^{2}	OR^{2}	—	—
Dumitrache	LCF	LCF	LCF	—	CF	CF	CF^{1}	LCF	CF	CF
Domide	—	—	RCF^{1}	—	—	—	—	—	—	RH^{2}
Lucescu	OL	OL^{1}	OL	LF	LF	LF^{1}	LF	—	—	—
Dumitrescu	—	—	—	—	—	—	—	OL	LF	RF

SCOTLAND

A	18. 4. 70	N. Ireland	0	Scotland (O'Hare)	1	Belfast (BHC)
B	22. 4. 70	Scotland	0	Wales	0	Glasgow (BHC)
C	25. 4. 70	Scotland	0	England	0	Glasgow (BHC)
D	11. 11. 70	Scotland (O'Hare)	1	Denmark	0	Glasgow (EFC)
E	3. 2. 71	Belgium (McKinnon o.g., Van Himst 2)	3	Scotland	0	Liege (EFC)

	*A	B	C	*D	E
Clark	G	—	—	—	—
Cruikshank	—	G	G	G	G
Hay	RB	CH	CH	RB^{1}	RB
Callaghan	—	RB	—	—	—
T. Gemmell	—	—	RB	—	LB
Jardine	—	—	—	RB^{2}	—
McKinnon	RCB	RCB	RCB	RCB	RCB
Moncur	LCB	LCB	LCB^{1}	LCB	LCB
Dickson	LB	LB	LB	—	—
Stanton	—	—	—	LB	RH^{1}
McLintock	LH	—	—	—	—
Gilzean	LCF^{1}	—	LCB^{2}	—	—
A. Gemmill	—	—	—	—	LH
McLean	OR	RF^{1}	—	—	—
Johnstone	—	—	RF	OR	—
Lennox	—	RF^{2}	—	—	—
Cooke	—	—	—	—	RF
O'Hare	RCF	CF	CF	RCF^{1}	LF
Stein	LCF^{2}	LF	LF	LCF	CF^{1}
Forest	—	—	—	—	CF^{2}

Carr	RH	LH	LH	RH	—	Cormack	—	—	—	RCF[2]	—
Greig	—	RH	RH	LH	CH	Johnston	OL	—	—	OL	—
Green	—	—	—	—	RH[2]						

SPAIN

A	11. 2. 70	Spain (Arieta 2)	2	West Germany	0	— Seville
B	22. 2. 70	Spain (Amancio, Salvadore o.g.)	2	Italy (Anastasi, Riva)	2	— Madrid
C	22. 4. 70	Switzerland	0	Spain (Rojo)	1	— Lausanne
D	28. 10. 70	Spain (Luis, Quini)	2	Greece (Papaioannou)	1	— Zaragoza
E	11. 11. 70	Spain (Rexach, Pirri, Luis)	3	N. Ireland	0	— Seville (EFC)
F	20. 2. 71	Italy (De Sisti)	1	Spain (Pirri, Uriarte)	2	— Cagliari
G	17. 3. 71	Spain (Pirri 2)	2	France (Revelli 2)	2	— Valencia

	*A	*B	*C	*D	E	F	G
Iribar	G	G	G	G	G	G	G
Sol	RB[1]	RB	RB	RCB[1]	RB[1]	RB	RB
Melo	RB[2]	—	—	RB	—	—	—
Hita	—	—	—	—	RB[2]	—	—
Gallego	RCB	RCB[1]	RCB	RCB[2]	RCB	RCB	RCB
Violeta	—	RCB[2]	LCB	—	RH	—	—
Costas	LCB	LCB[1]	—	LCB	LCB	LCB	RH[1]
Eladio	LB	LB	LB	—	—	—	—
Adelardo	—	—	—	LB	—	—	—
Rife	—	—	—	—	LB	—	—
Tonono	—	—	—	—	—	LB	LCB
Arieta	RH	LCF	LCF[1]	—	RF	CF[2]	CF[1]
Lora	LH	RH	RH	—	CF[2]	—	RH[2]
Rodilla	—	—	—	LH[2]	—	—	—
Pirri	—	—	—	—	LH	CH	CH
Luis	—	—	—	OR	CH	—	—
Claramunt	—	—	—	—	—	RH	LH
Amancio	OR	OR	OR	LH[1]	—	RF[1]	RF[1]
Garate	RCF[1]	RCF	RCF[1]	RCF[1]	—	CF[1]	—
Ufarte	RCF[2]	—	—	—	—	—	—
Quini	—	—	—	RCF[2]	CF[1]	—	CF[2]
Grosso	—	LCB[2]	LCF[2]	—	—	—	—
Marcial	—	—	—	LCF	—	RF[2]	—
Asensi	—	—	RCF[2]	—	—	—	—
Rojo	OL	OL	OL	—	—	—	—
Uriate	LCF	LH	LH	RH	—	LH	—
Rexach	—	—	—	OL	LF	—	RF[2]
Churruca	—	—	—	—	—	LF	LF
Anton	—	—	—	—	—	—	LB

SWEDEN

A	22. 2. 70	Mexico	0	Sweden	0	— Mexico City
B	1. 3. 70	Mexico	0	Sweden (Eriksson)	1	— Puebla
C	17. 5. 70	Hungary (Fazekas)	1	Sweden (Persson, Eiderstedt)	2	— Budapest
D	3. 6. 70	Italy (Domenghini)	1	Sweden	0	— Toluca (WC)
E	7. 6. 70	Sweden (Turesson)	1	Israel (Spiegel)	1	— Toluca (WC)

F	10. 6. 70	Sweden (Grahn)	1	Uruguay	0	Puebla (WC)
G	25. 6. 70	Sweden (Palsson)	1	Denmark (K. Petersen)	1	Gothenburg
H	26. 8. 70	Finland (Lindholm)	1	Sweden (Almqvist, Brzokopil)	2	Helsinki
I	13. 9. 70	Norway (Nilsen, Fugset)	2	Sweden (Danielsson, Brzokopil, Svensson 2)	4	Oslo
J	14. 10. 70	Rep. of Ireland (Carroll)	1	Sweden (Brzokopil)	1	Dublin (EFC)
K	28. 10. 70	Sweden (Turesson)	1	Rep. of Ireland	0	Stockholm (EFC)

	A	B	C	D	E	F	G	H	*I	J	K
Hellstrom	G	G	G[1]	G	—	—	—	—	—	—	G
S-G. Larsson	—	—	G[2]	—	G	G	G	G	G	G	—
Selander	RB	RB[1]	RB	—	RB	RB	RB	RB	RB	RB	RB
Cronquist	RF[2]	RB[2]	—	RB	—	—	—	LCB	—	—	LB[2]
Kristensson	RCB	RCB	RCB[2]	—	—	—	—	RCB	RCB	RCB	RCB
Axelsson	—	—	RCB[1]	RCB	RCB	RCB	RCB	—	—	—	—
Nordqvist	LCB	LCB	LCB	LCB	—	LCB	LCB	—	LCB	LCB	LCB
Grip	LB	LB	LB	LB	LB	LB	LB	LB	LB	LB	LB[1]
Svensson	RH	RH	RH	RH	RH	RH	RH[1]	RH	RH	RH	RH
Eriksson	CH	CH	CH	CH[1]	—	CH	RF[1]	CH	RCF	RF	RF
Olsson	—	—	—	LF	LCB	—	CF	—	—	CH	CH
Bo Larsson	LH	LH	LH	LH[1]	LH	LH	LH	LH	LH	LH	LH
Danielsson	RF[1]	RF[1]	—	—	—	—	—	RF	OR	CF[1]	—
Kindvall	—	—	—	RF	RF	RF[1]	—	—	—	—	—
Eiderstedt	CF[1]	CF[2]	RF	CH[2]	—	—	RF[2]	—	—	—	—
G. Nicklasson	LF	RF[2]	—	LH[2]	—	CF[1]	CH	—	—	—	—
Palsson	CF[2]	LF	—	—	LF[2]	—	RH[2]	—	—	—	—
Eklund	—	CF[1]	—	—	—	—	—	—	LCF[2]	—	—
Nordahl	—	—	CF[1]	—	CH	—	—	—	—	—	—
Turesson	—	—	CF[2]	—	CF	RF[2]	—	—	—	—	CF[2]
Brzokopil	—	—	—	—	—	—	—	CF[2]	OL	CF[2]	CF[1]
Almqvist	—	—	—	—	—	—	—	CF[1]	—	—	—
Persson	—	—	LF	—	LF[1]	LF	LF	—	—	—	—
Grahn	—	—	—	CF	—	CF[2]	—	—	—	LF	LF
Nordin	—	—	—	—	—	—	—	—	LCF[1]	—	—
Johansson	—	—	—	—	—	—	—	LF[1]	—	—	—
C. Nicklasson	—	—	—	—	—	—	—	LF[2]	—	—	—

WALES

A	18. 4. 70	Wales (Krzywicki)	1	England (Lee)	1	Cardiff (BHC)
B	22. 4. 70	Scotland	0	Wales	0	Glasgow (BHC)
C	25. 4. 70	Wales (Rees)	1	N. Ireland	0	Swansea (BHC)
D	11. 11. 70	Wales	0	Rumania	0	Cardiff (EFC)

	A	B	C	D
Millington	G	G	G	—
Sprake	—	—	—	G
Rodriques	RB	RB	RB	RB
England	RCB	RCB	RCB	RCB
Powell	LCB	LCB	LCB	LCB
Thomas	LB	LB	LB	LB
Hennessey	RH	RH	RH	—
Hole	—	—	—	RH
Durban	CH	CH	CH	CH
Moore	LH	LH	LH	LH
Krzywicki	RF	RF	RF	RF
Ron Davies	CF	CF	CF	—
Wyn Davies	—	—	—	CF
Rees	LF	LF	LF	LF